1/80

D0325876

Civilized Man's Eight Deadly Sins

Civilized Man's Eight Deadly Sins

Konrad Lorenz

Translated by Marjorie Kerr Wilson

A Helen and Kurt Wolff Book

Harcourt Brace Jovanovich, Inc.

New York

Copyright © 1973 by R. Piper & Co. Verlag
English translation copyright © 1974 by Konrad Lorenz

All rights reserved. No part of this publication may
be reproduced or transmitted in any form or by any means,
electronic or mechanical, including photocopy, recording,
or any information storage and retrieval system,
without permission in writing from the publisher.

Printed in the United States of America

Library of Congress Cataloging in Publication Data

Lorenz, Konrad.
        Civilized man's eight deadly sins.

        "A Helen and Kurt Wolff book."
        Translation of Die acht Todsünden der zivilisierten
Menschheit.
        Bibliography: p.
        1. Human ecology—Addresses, essays, lectures.
2. Civilization, Modern—Addresses, essays, lectures.
I. Title.
GF41.L6713   301.31   73–20189
ISBN 0–15–118061–X

First edition
B C D E

Contents

88927

A Foreword with
a Silver Lining

During the final stages of publishing a paper or a book, I always feel strongly repelled by my own writing. Not that it seems scientifically wrong, but it appears increasingly hackneyed and banal and less worth publishing. At last my revulsion reaches such an intensity that, when it comes to reading galley proofs, I always feel reminded of an awful sight once seen in a prisoner-of-war camp: a man slowly and deliberately eating his own vomit.

My aversion wears off with time, and after a few years or so I do not feel so bad about my products; at least they do not seem any more to be worse than other people's writings. So I like to think that this later view is more objective than the first one had been.

These labor pains are less tormenting in the publishing of a translation. In the guise of a good translation one's own book appears to be—as it actually is—another person's work, and as such it affords a new viewpoint from which to judge it more objectively. It was, therefore, all the more disquieting when, in reading this translation, I was haunted by the feeling that something

was subtly wrong with this book, though I could not at
first put my finger on it.

I have since found out: it is the attitude that I myself
took while writing this book only four years ago. The
tone of the book makes it all too obvious that the author
feels like a prophet crying in the wilderness, and that
kind of prophet is not an altogether likable person. For
one thing, he is offended by the fact that no human being
is listening to his crying, and therefore he always sounds
slightly reproachful. Furthermore, he is talking *down* to
his audience, which is forgivable, since he believes it to
consist only of wilderness animals.

This prophet-in-the-wilderness attitude was wrong in
the first place; it was obsolete when I first wrote this
book. It was more out-of-date when it was made accessi-
ble to the public, and it is even more so at the present
moment. After holding what I thought to be more or less
a monologue in the wilderness, I found that I had been
talking to an intelligent and appreciative audience—a
double-edged experience, highly satisfactory and highly
embarrassing at the same time. I apologize in advance if
ever I seem to be "talking down" to the reader.

In still another way the tone of the book is slightly
wrong: it is too pessimistic. Only a few years ago, those
who raised their voices to warn humanity about the dangers threatening it from its own shortsightedness really
were prophets crying in the wilderness. I myself must
plead guilty of having regarded William Vogt, the ecol-
ogist, as unduly pessimistic. Rachel Carson was thought
so by many people, and no effective protests were raised

when the producers of poison tried most unfairly to discredit her and to hound her into oblivion. Today everybody regards her as a martyr, and nobody doubts that her predictions were accurate.

True, the dangers threatening humanity have in no way diminished, but the number of people who are aware of them is rapidly increasing. The dark clouds are threatening, coming closer and closer, but they have a silver lining which, though narrow enough, is increasing in luminescence. True, a dark cloud of collective stupidity is still obscuring the minds of many influential people. It is still possible that men who ought to know better regard the report on the limits of growth made by M.I.T. at the request of the Club of Rome as sheer irresponsible nonsense; incredibly, they even find journals to print what *really is* sheer irresponsible nonsense. But, in general, awareness of humanity's predicament is spreading with exponentially increasing speed. It *needs to,* because the dangers are doing exactly the same. It is a neck-and-neck race between the growing of the cloud and the broadening of the silver lining. However, I am *not* without hope; in fact, I would not work on this book if I were.

Furthermore, I am very glad to state that I have to qualify quite a few things that are said in Europe about America. It is still true that the United States is the worst sinner in regard to air and water pollution, as well as in respect to the exponential growth of production and consumption. But it is equally true that America is the land in which the greatest number of responsible men and women are really concerned about the predicaments of humanity; it is in America that the warnings of Carson, Vogt, Philip Wylie, the Meadows team, and many others were first heard. If the great errors of our Western civilization are usually first committed in America, it is also the country in which these errors are first recognized and corrected. A good example of this is the indoctrination of America with the teachings of behaviorism. In this book, on page 49, I complain about the devastating moral and intellectual influence that behavioristic doctrine is exerting on American public opinion, as well as on psychological and sociological science. Now I can see signs that this is not so any more, while in Europe the behaviorist's influence is still expanding.

I feel that I should give some justification for my writing the kind of sermon contained in this book. To do so is not generally considered the task of the scientist. However, in medical science it is legitimate to give warning whenever there is reason to suspect a threatening illness, even if its cause is not yet fully analyzed. This is indubitably the case with many of the epidemic mental illnesses afflicting present-day humanity.

I want to conclude this foreword by reiterating my avowal of optimism. It would be unpardonably arrogant to believe that the facts one can plainly understand oneself cannot be made intelligible to all and sundry. Everything that follows is far easier to understand than integral or differential calculus (which I never quite mastered, though I understand the principle). Every danger loses some of its terror once its causes are understood. Many neuroses can actually be cured by raising their deep, subconscious roots above the level of consciousness. In respect to both these facts I dare hope that my little book might contribute to a slight lessening of the dangers that are threatening us.

Civilized Man's
Eight Deadly Sins

One

Structural Properties
and Functional Disorders
of Living Systems

Ethology may be defined as that branch of science which arose when the comparative methods, obligatory since Darwin in all other biological disciplines, were applied also to research into animal and human behavior. The surprising lateness of this application was due to the sequence of events in the history of behavior research, which I will deal with in the section on indoctrination. Ethology treats animal and human behavior as the function of a system owing its existence, as well as its special form, to a development process that has taken place in the history of the species, in the development of the individual and, in man, in cultural history. The genuine causal question, *why* a certain system is constructed in a certain manner, and not otherwise, can find its legitimate answer only in the natural explanation of this evolutionary process.

Among the causes of all organic evolution, next to the processes of mutation and new combination of genes, the biggest part is played by natural selection. It brings about *adaptation,* a genuine cognitive process by which the organism absorbs information about the environment, significant for its survival; in other words, it acquires *knowledge* of the environment.

The presence of structures and functions formed by adaptation is characteristic of living organisms; in the inorganic world there is nothing of this kind. This fact compels the natural scientist to ask a question, unknown to the physicist and the chemist, the question "What for?" When the biologist asks this, he is searching not for the teleological significance but, more modestly, for the survival value of a characteristic. When we ask, "What does the cat have curved, pointed claws for?" and answer, "For catching mice," we are simply asking which survival function has bred this form of claw in the cat.

Having spent a scientist's lifetime asking this question about the strangest structures and behavior patterns over and over again, and finding, over and over again, a convincing answer, one tends to the view that complex and by and large improbable forms of body structure and behavior come into being exclusively through selection and adaptation. That view, however, would be completely shaken if the question "What for?" were applied to certain regularly observable behavior patterns of civilized human beings. What is the use to humanity of its measureless multiplication, its mad competitive haste, its production of ever deadlier weapons, the progressive deterioration of town dwellers, and so on. A closer view shows that virtually all these malfunctions are disorders of certain special behavior mechanisms, originally possessing survival value. In other words, the disorders are *pathological.*

The analysis of the organic system underlying the social behavior of man is the most difficult and ambitious task that the scientist can set himself, for this system is by far the most complex on earth. One might imagine that an undertaking of such intrinsic difficulty would be rendered altogether impossible by the fact that human behavior is overlaid and altered unpredictably by pathological phenomena. Fortunately, this is not the case. Far from being an insurmountable obstacle to the analysis of an organic system, a pathological disorder is often the key to understanding it. We know of many cases in the history of physiology where a scientist became aware of an important organic system only after a pathological disturbance had caused its disease. When E. T. Kocher treated exophthalmic goiter by excision of the thyroid, he initially produced tetany because, with the thyroid, he had removed the parathyroid glands, the regulators of calcium metabolism. Having corrected this mistake, he elicited, by the still too radical removal of the thyroid, a syndrome that he called cachexia thyreopriva, which showed certain resemblances to myxoedema, a form of idiocy occurring frequently in Alpine valleys, where the water is deficient in iodine. From these and similar results, it was found that the endocrine glands form a system in which, quite literally, everything is linked to everything else in causal interaction. Every secretion poured into the body by the endocrine glands has a definite action on the whole organism, influencing metabolism, growth, behavior, and so on. These secretions are therefore called hormones (from Greek *hormaein:* to urge on). The actions of two hormones may be exactly antagonistic, in a way analogous to the actions of two muscles which, by opposing play, bring a joint into the desired position and keep it there. As long as hormonal equilibrium is maintained, it is not apparent that the endocrine system is built up of part functions, but if the harmony of actions and reactions is in the least upset, the whole condition of the organism diverges from the desired theoretical norm, *i.e.*, it becomes diseased. Too much thyroid causes exophthalmic goiter, too little, myxoedema.

The endocrine system and the history of its investigation provide us with valuable aids to the understanding of the whole system of human impulses. Obviously, this system is much more complexly structured, and must be so since it encompasses the endocrine glands as a subsystem. Man evidently possesses a great many independent sources of impulses, and a large number of these may be attributed to behavior programs of phylogenetic origin, to "instincts." It is misleading to call man the "instinct-reduction being," as I did in the past. It is true that in the course of phylogenetic higher evolution of learning ability and insight, long, coherent chains of innate behavior patterns can "dissolve"; the obligatory links between their parts get lost, whereupon these fragments become independently available to the acting subject. P. Leyhausen has demonstrated this convincingly in his experiments with cats. At the same time, as Leyhausen showed, every one of these available fragments becomes an autonomous drive, since it develops an appetitive behavior striving for its discharge. Unquestionably, man lacks long chains of obligatorily linked instinctive movements, but so far as we may dare to extrapolate from findings in highly developed mammals, we may assume that man has not fewer but more genuinely instinctive impulses than any other animal. In any case, when attempting system analysis, we must take into account this possibility.

This is particularly important in the examination of behavior that is obviously pathologically disturbed. My late friend, the psychiatrist Ronald Hargreaves, in one of his last letters to me, wrote that when trying to understand a mental disorder, he had made it his method to ask *two* questions: first, what is the normal survival function of the disturbed system and, second, what is the nature of the disturbance, in particular whether it has been caused by an over- or an underfunction of a part system. The part systems of a complex organic whole exist in a state of such intimate interaction that it is hard to draw a line between their several functions, none of which in its normal form is conceivable without all the others. Not even the structures of part systems are always clearly definable. This is what Paul Weiss means when, in his "The Living System: Determinism Strati-

fied," he says of subordinate systems that a system is
everything which is uniform enough to deserve a name.

There are a great many human impulses uniform
enough to have been given a name in colloquial language. Words like hate, love, friendship, anger, loyalty,
affection, mistrust, trust, and so on, all signify states
corresponding with the propensity to quite specific behavior patterns, in a way no different from the terms applied in scientific behavior research, such as aggressivity, ranking-order drive, territoriality, and termini
connected with "mood," for example, brooding, court-
ing, or flying mood. We trust the "flair" of natural expression for deep psychological associations as much as
the intuition of scientific animal observers, and we may
assume—at first only as a working hypothesis—that every one of these terms for human states of mind and for
certain actions corresponds with a real impulse system.
For the present it is immaterial in what proportions the
particular impulse derives its force from phylogenetic
or from cultural sources. We may assume that every one
of these impulses is a link in a well-ordered, harmoni-
ously working system and, as such, indispensable. The
question whether hate, love, trust, mistrust, and so on,
are "good" or "bad," if asked without understanding of
the systemic function of this whole, is just as stupid as
the question whether the thyroid gland is good or bad.
The idea that emotions can be classified as good and
bad, that love, loyalty, and trust are good in themselves,
while hate, disloyalty, and mistrust are bad, stems from
the fact that in our society there is generally a lack of

the former and a surfeit of the latter. Too much love spoils countless promising children, too much loyalty, raised to an absolute, has had appalling consequences, and Erik Erikson has recently demonstrated convincingly the indispensability of mistrust.

One structural property common to all more highly integrated systems is that of regulation by so-called feedback cycles or homeostases. In order to understand their action, we must imagine a working structure, consisting of a number of systems supporting each other functionally in such a way that system A sustains the action of B, B that of C, and so on, until finally Z supports the function of A. Such a cycle of "positive feedback" is, at best, in a state of unstable equilibrium; the smallest increase of a single action will lead to snowballing of all the system functions, and, conversely, the slightest decrease to the ebbing of all activity. As technology has long known, such an unstable system can be converted to a stable one by introducing into the cycle a single link whose action on the subsequent one in the chain of effects decreases in proportion to the increase in strength exerted by the link preceding it. Thus a regulating cycle is set up, a homeostasis or "negative feedback." It is one of the few processes that was discovered by technologists before it was detected by biologists in the realm of the organic.

In nature, there are countless regulating cycles. They are so indispensable for the preservation of life that we can scarcely imagine its origin without the simultaneous "invention" of the regulating cycle. Cycles of positive feedback are hardly ever found in nature, or, at most, in a rapidly waxing and just as rapidly waning process such as an avalanche or a prairie fire. These phenomena resemble various pathological disorders of human society.

The negative feedback of the regulating cycle dispenses with the necessity of a specific fixed measure—the action of every single one of the subsystems participating in it. A small over- or underfunction is easily equilibrated, and a dangerous upset of the whole system occurs only if a part function increases or decreases to such a degree that the homeostasis can no longer be equilibrated, or, if the regulating mechanism itself is out of order. In the following chapters we will meet with examples of both these conditions.

Two

Overpopulation

In the single organism, we almost never come across a positive feedback cycle. Only life as a whole can indulge with apparent impunity in this immoderation. Organic life has built itself, like a rare kind of dam, into the stream of dissipating world energy; it "devours" negative entropy, gathers energy voraciously, and grows with it. Moreover, the process of growth enables it to acquire more and more energy, and all the more quickly, the more it has already gathered in. If this process has not yet led to overproliferation and to catastrophe, it is because the merciless powers of the inorganic, the laws of probability, keep the multiplication of living beings within bounds, and also because regulating cycles have been formed between the different species of living organisms. In the next chapter, which deals with the destruction of our earthly environment, we shall explain briefly how these cycles work. We must discuss the measureless multiplication of human beings first, since it is the cause of most of the phenomena that are the subjects of our later consideration.

All those gifts that have sprung from man's deep insight into the nature of his surroundings—the progress of his technology, his chemical and medical sciences, everything that seems most likely to relieve human suffering—work in a horrible and paradoxical way toward the destruction of mankind. And humanity threatens to do what living systems almost never do, namely to suffocate in itself. Worst of all, in this apocalypse, the highest and noblest properties and faculties of man, the ones rightly valued as specifically human, are apparently the first to perish. We who live in densely populated civilized countries, especially in large cities, no longer realize how much we are in want of warm-hearted human affection. You have to go to a really sparsely populated country, where neighbors are separated by several miles of bad roads, and enter a house uninvited, to realize how hospitable and friendly people are when their capacity for social contact is not continually overstrained.

This was brought home to me by an unforgettable experience. We had an American couple staying with us in Austria whose house is situated in an isolated spot in the woods of Wisconsin. Just as we were sitting down to dinner, the doorbell rang and I cried out angrily, "Who on earth is that now?" I could not have shocked my visitors more if I had let fly a volley of obscene oaths. To them it was inconceivable that anyone could react to the ringing of the bell with anything but pleasure.

Crowded together in our huge modern cities, in the

phantasmagoria of human faces, superimposed on each other and blurred, we no longer see the face of our neighbor. Our neighborly love becomes so diluted by a surfeit of neighbors that, in the end, not a trace of it is left. Anyone who still wants to feel affection for his fellow humans must concentrate it on a small number of friends, for we are not so constituted that we can love all mankind, however right and ethical the exhortation to do so may be. So we must select, that is, we must keep certain people, who would be fully worthy of our friendship, at a distance. "Not to get emotionally involved" is one of the chief worries of large-city people. This state of affairs, not quite avoidable for any of us, already bears the stamp of *inhumanity;* it is redolent of the old American plantation owners who treated their "house niggers" as human beings but their plantation slaves at best as valuable domestic animals. When this intentional screening-off from human contacts goes further, it leads not only to emotional entropy, of which I will speak later, but to the horrible manifestations of apathy reported daily in the press. The greater the overcrowding, the more urgent becomes the need for the individual "not to get involved"; thus, today, in the largest cities, robbery, murder, and rape take place in broad daylight, and in crowded streets, without the intervention of any passer-by.

The overcrowding of many people into a small space leads, not only indirectly through exhaustion of interhuman relationships, but also directly, to aggressive behavior. Animal experiments have shown that intraspecific aggression can be escalated by overcrowding. Nobody, who has not been a prisoner of war or personally experienced a similar compulsory aggregation of human beings, can imagine what pitch the smallest irritation can reach under such circumstances. When, in daily and hourly contact with fellow humans who are not our friends, we continually try to be polite and friendly, our state of mind becomes unbearable. The general unfriendliness, evident in all large cities, is clearly proportional to the density of human masses in certain places. For example, in large railway stations and at the bus terminal in New York City, it reaches a frightening intensity.

Indirectly, overcrowding contributes toward all the symptoms of decay that we will be discussing in the following chapters. The idea that by suitable "conditioning" a new kind of human being, immune to the effects of dense overcrowding, could be produced, is, to my mind, a dangerous madness.

Three

Devastation of
the Environment

It is a widespread but erroneous belief that "nature" is inexhaustible. Every species of animal, plant, or fungus —for all three are part of an intricate mechanism—is adapted to its environment, and to this environment belong not only the inorganic parts of a certain habitat but also all the other living inhabitants. Thus all the living beings of a habitat are adapted to *each other,* and this applies also to those confronting each other in apparent hostility, for example, the predator and its prey, the eater and the eaten. On closer consideration, it is evident that these beings, seen as species and not as individuals, not only do not harm each other but even form a mutual-interest society. Obviously, the eater has a strong interest in the ongoing existence of the species he lives by, whether it be animal or plant, and the more specialized he is in a certain kind of nourishment, the greater his interest in its survival. In such cases, the predator is unable ever to exterminate the prey species, for the last pair of predators would starve long before it even encountered the last pair of prey animals. If the population density of the prey species falls below a certain level, the predator ceases to exist, just as, fortunately, most whaling concerns have done. When the dingo, originally a domestic dog, came to Australia and ran wild there, it did not eliminate any of the prey species that it lived on; instead, it exterminated both the large marsupial predators, the marsupial wolf, *Thylacynus*, and the Tasmanian devil, *Sarcophilus*. These marsupials, armed with terrible teeth, were infinitely superior to the dingo as fighters but, because of their primitive brain, they required a much denser population of prey animals than the more intelligent wild dog. They were not bitten to death by the dingo but killed in competition—they starved.

It is rare for the multiplication of an animal species to be regulated directly by the amount of available nourishment. This would be uneconomical for the predator as well as for the prey. A fisherman living off certain fishing grounds will be well advised to exploit them only so far that the surviving fish can reproduce sufficiently to make up for the fish caught. Where this optimum lies can be worked out only by a very complicated maximim-minimum calculation: should we fish too little, the sea will remain overpopulated and not many young will mature; should we overfish, too few will be left to breed the number of progeny that the area can properly nourish. As V. C. Wynne-Edwards has shown in his book, *Animal Dispersion in Relation to*

Social Behaviour, many animal species practice an analogous kind of economy. As well as the marking of territories to preclude too close aggregation, there are various other behavior patterns calculated to prevent overexploitation of the available environment.

Quite frequently, the eaten species gains advantages from the eater. Not only is the reproduction rate of nutritive plants and animals adapted to the consumer, so that a vital equilibrium would be upset if this factor were obliterated. (The great breakdowns of population seen in quickly breeding rodents immediately after their attaining highest population densities endanger the survival of the species much more than does "culling" by predators, which helps to preserve a balanced medium.) The symbiosis often goes much further. There are many grasses "constructed" to be kept short and even trampled down by large ungulates. In our lawns, we imitate this process by mowing and rolling. If these factors disappear, these grass species are soon supplanted by others that have been unable to stand up to such treatment but are hardier in other ways. In short, two life forms can have the same relationship of interdependence that exists between man and his domestic animals and plants. The laws governing such interactions are often similar to those of human economy, a fact expressed in the biological term for the science of these interactions: ecology. However, *one* economical concept, about which we shall have more to say later, does not occur in the ecology of animals and plants: overexploitation of natural resources.

The interactions of the many animal, plant, and fungus species coexisting in a habitat and forming a common life society, or biocoenosis, are manifold and complex. The adaptation of different species of living beings, produced during periods whose size order corresponds with geological rather than with historical epochs, has led to a state of equilibrium as expedient as it is unstable. Many regulating processes support this equilibrium against the inevitable disturbances caused by weather and similar influences. Slowly occurring changes wrought by evolution or gradual alterations of climate cannot endanger the balance of a habitat, but sudden influences, even if apparently slight, may have catastrophic effects. The introduction of a seemingly harmless animal species can devastate wide stretches of land, as rabbits have done in Australia. This interference in the balance of a biotope was caused by man. Similar ravages may be brought about without his interference, but this is rarer.

The ecology of man changes much more rapidly than that of other creatures, and the speed of its change is dictated by his technological progress, which keeps accelerating in a geometrical progression. Thus man cannot avoid making fundamental changes, and, all too often, he causes the total breakdown of the biocoenosis in which and on which he lives. Exceptions to this rule are seen in a few "wild" tribes, for example, certain South American jungle Indians who live as gatherers and hunters; also in the inhabitants of several oceanic islands, who carry on some agriculture but otherwise live on coconuts and sea animals. Such human cultures influence their biotopes in a way no different from that of populations of animal species. This is the one theoretically possible way in which man can live in equilibrium with his biotope; the other way is by *creating*, through crop growing and animal breeding, a new biocoenosis, tailored to suit his needs and, in principle, just as viable as one that has arisen without his help. A biocoenosis of this kind may be seen in many old farms, where, for generations, the same families have lived on the same land; they are one with it and, having sound ecological knowledge acquired by experience, they give back to the soil what they have taken from it.

The farmer knows something that the whole of civilized mankind seems to have forgotten, namely, that the resources of life on our planet are *not inexhaustible.* In the United States, it was only after wide expanses of plowland had been eroded through ruthless exploitation of the top soil, after large districts had been devastated by timbering, and countless useful animal species had become extinct that these facts gradually began to be realized again, particularly because many large agricultural, fishing, and whaling industries began to feel the effects financially. Nevertheless, the truth has only begun to penetrate to the consciousness of the general public.

Present-day haste leaves people no time to think before they act. They are proud of being "doers," little suspecting that they are the undoers of nature and themselves. Everywhere there is undoing: in the use of chemicals in agriculture and horticulture and, just as shortsightedly, in pharmacy. Immunity biologists are gravely concerned about the general misuse of medicaments. Several branches of the chemical industry unscrupulously exploit the psychology of "instant gratification" by the sale of products whose delayed action cannot yet be assessed. There is an appalling lack of foresight about the future of agriculture and medicine. Those who have warned against the indiscriminate use of insecticides, herbicides, and chemical preservatives have been discredited and silenced in an infamous way.

When civilized man destroys in blind vandalism the natural habitat surrounding and sustaining him, he threatens himself with ecological ruin. Once he begins to feel this economically, he will probably realize his mistakes, but by then it may be too late. Least of all does he notice how much this barbarian process damages his own mind. The general, fast-spreading alienation from nature can largely be blamed on the increasing aesthetic and ethical vulgarity that characterizes civilized mankind. How can one expect a sense of reverential awe for anything in the young when all they see around them is man-made and the cheapest and ugliest of its kind. For the city dweller, even the view of the sky is obscured by skyscrapers and chemical clouding of the atmosphere. No wonder the progress of civilization goes hand in hand with the deplorable disfigurement of town and country.

If we compare the old center of any European town

with its modern periphery, or compare this periphery, this cultural horror, eating its way into the surrounding countryside, with the still unspoiled villages, and then compare a histological picture of any normal body tissue with that of a malignant tumor, we find astonishing analogies. Considered objectively, and translated from the aesthetic to the computable, this difference consists essentially in a *loss of information*. The cell of the malignant tumor differs from the normal body cell in that it has lost all the genetical information it requires in order to be able to play its part as a useful member of the body's cell community. Therefore the malignant cell behaves like a unicellular animal or a young embryonic cell. It lacks special structures and multiplies ruthlessly, so that the tumor tissue infiltrates the still healthy neighboring tissue and destroys it. The similarities between the two processes are obvious. In both cases, the still sound parts contain highly differentiated and mutually complementary structures that owe their symmetry to information gathered in the course of a long evolution; whereas, in the tumor, or in modern technology, only very few extremely simple structures dominate the picture. The histological picture of the completely uniform, structurally poor tumor tissue has a frightening resemblance to an aerial view of a modern suburb with its monotonous houses designed by architects without much art, without much thought, and in the haste of competition. The processes involved in the race of mankind with itself, the subject of the next chapter, have a devastating effect on house building. Because of the commercial consideration that mass-produced building parts are cheaper, and also because of fashion, that leveler of all things, on all town outskirts in all civilized countries, mass dwellings are springing up by the thousands. Indistinguishable from each other except by numbers, and unworthy of the name "houses," they are at best batteries for "utility people," to use an expression analogous to the term "utility animals."

Keeping hens in batteries is rightly looked upon as cruelty to animals and a disgrace to civilization, but nobody objects to a similar confinement of humans, even though man can stand this literally inhuman treatment even less than animals. The self-valuation of the normal person rightly demands that he should be allowed to express his individuality. A man is not, like an ant or a termite, constructed phylogenetically in such a way that he can bear being an anonymous and interchangeable element among millions of absolutely similar others. One has only to look at a row of gardens to see how strong is man's impulse to assert his personality. The dweller in the utility battery has only one way of keeping up his self-respect: by banishing the existence of his many fellow sufferers from his consciousness and encapsulating himself from his neighbors. In many mass-produced apartment houses, partitions have been erected between the balconies to make the neighbor invisible. One cannot, and will not, come in contact with him "across the fence," for one is afraid of seeing one's own frustrated face reflected in his. In this way, living in masses leads to loneliness and to apathy toward one's neighbor.

Aesthetic and ethical feeling appear to be closely related, and people who are obliged to live under the conditions described above obviously suffer from an atrophy of both. It seems that both the beauty of nature and the beauty of cultural surroundings created by man are necessary to keep people mentally healthy. The complete blindness to everything beautiful, so common in these times, is a mental illness that must be taken seriously for the simple reason that it goes hand in hand with insensitivity to the ethically wrong.

In the case of the people who have to decide whether a street, a power station or a factory should be built, destroying forever the beauty of a whole stretch of land, ethical considerations play no part whatever. From the chairman of a small rural council to the minister of economics in a large state, all are unanimous that no economic—or indeed political—sacrifice must be made to nature. The few nature lovers and scientists whose eyes are open to the impending disaster are powerless: a piece of land belonging to a rural council will fetch a better price if a new road is made; and so the bubbling brook, winding its way through the village, is diverted throught a conduit, and the pretty country lane becomes a dreary suburban street.

Four

Man's Race
Against Himself

At the beginning of Chapter 1, I have explained why, in the living system, the function of regulating cycles or negative feedback is indispensable for the maintenance of a steady state; also why positive feedback cycles always threaten to trigger the snowballing of a single action. A special case of positive feedback occurs when individuals of the same species enter into a competition with each other which, through selection, influences their evolution. In contrast to selection caused by extraspecific environmental factors, *intraspecific* selection effects, in the species concerned, changes in the hereditary pattern that not only do not enhance its survival chances but in most cases are detrimental to them.

To illustrate the consequences of intraspecific selection, my teacher Oskar Heinroth chose the example of the secondary feathers of the Argus cock pheasant, *Argusianus argus L.* In courtship, these are spread and presented to the hen in a way analogous to that of the peacock's tail, which is formed by the upper tail coverts. Just as in the peacock, so in the Argus, too, the choice of the partner evidently rests with the hen, and the mating chances of the cock are in fairly direct relation to the degree of attraction exerted on the hen by the male courtship organ. In flight, however, the peacock's tail is folded into a more or less streamlined stern and is scarcely a hindrance, whereas the elongated secondaries of the male Argus render him almost incapable of flight. That he has not become entirely so is obviously due to the fact that ground predators exert a selection pressure in the opposite direction, thereby bringing about the necessary regulating effect.

Oskar Heinroth, in his drastic manner, used to say, "After the wings of the Argus cock, the working pace of modern man is the stupidest product of intraspecific selection." At the time it was made, this assertion was surely prophetical. Today it is a classical understatement. In the Argus, as in many other animals with similar structures, environmental influences prevent the species from moving, by intraspecific selection, along monstrous evolutionary paths leading to catastrophe. No such salubrious regulating forces are at work in the cultural evolution of mankind. To his detriment, man has learned to govern all the forces of his extraspecific environment, but he knows so little about himself that he is helplessly at the mercy of the satanic workings of intraspecific selection.

Homo homini lupus—"Man is the predator of man" is, like Heinroth's saw, an understatement. Man, as the only determining selection factor in the further evolution of his own species, is, unfortunately, in no way so harmless as even the most dangerous beast of prey. As no biological factor has ever done before, the competition between man and man works in direct opposition to all the forces of nature, destroying nearly all the values these have created, with a cold calculation dictated exclusively by value-blind commercial considerations.

Under the pressure of interhuman competition, all that is good and useful, for humanity as a whole as well as for the individual human being, has been completely set aside. The overwhelming majority of people today value only that which brings commercial gain and is calculated to outflank fellow humans in the relentless race of competition. Every means serving this end appears, falsely, as a value in itself. Utilitarianism, with its destructive influence, may be defined as the mistaking of the means for the end. Money is a means. Colloquial language expresses this: we say, "He has the means." How many people today would understand if we tried to explain that money by itself does not represent any value? The same applies to time: the saying "Time is money" means, to all those for whom money is an absolute value, that every second of saved time represents an equivalent worth. If we build airplanes to fly the Atlantic in ever-decreasing time spans, nobody asks what price we have paid for the necessary lengthening of the runway, for the greater speed of take-off and landing with all the associated greater risks, and for the volume of noise involved. The general opinion will be that the saving of half an hour is a value in itself and that no sacrifice can be too great in achieving it. Every car manufacturer must take care that the newest model is a little faster than the one before; every road must be widened; every corner enlarged, ostensibly in the interests of safety but in reality so that we can drive still faster—and more recklessly.

We must ask ourselves what does more damage to the mind of modern man: his blinding greed for money or his enervating haste. Whichever of the two it may be, it is clearly the intention of the governing powers, irrespective of their political ideology, to further them both and to stimulate, to the extent of hypertrophy, every motivation that drives people to compete. As far as I know, no deep psychological analysis of this motivation has been made, but, in my opinion, it is very probable that, beside greed for property or for higher social standing, or both, *fear* plays an essential role—fear of being overtaken in the race, fear of poverty, fear of making wrong decisions, fear of not being able to keep up with the whole nerve-racking situation. Anxiety in every form is certainly the basic factor undermining the health of modern man, causing high blood pressure, renal atrophy, cardiac infarction and other diseases. Man rushes, not only because he is propelled by greed, for this alone would not induce him to ruin his own health, but because he is *driven*, and what drives him can only be fear.

Anxious haste and hasty fear help to rob man of his most essential properties. One of these is *reflection*. In my work *Innate Bases of Learning,* I have described how, in the mysterious process of becoming man, a decisive part was probably played by the fact that one day a creature inquisitively exploring its environment became aware of its own self in the field of its vision. This discovery of the self need not necessarily have arisen side by side with that astonishment at the hitherto taken-for-granted, which is the birth act of philosophy. The mere fact that the groping and grasping hand, besides the groped for and grasped extraneous object, was seen and understood as a thing of the outside world, must have formed a new association, the effects of which were epoch-making. A being unaware of the existence of its own self cannot possibly develop conceptual thought, word language, conscience, and responsible morality. A being that *ceases* to reflect is in danger of losing all these specifically human attributes.

One of the worst effects of haste, or of the fear engendered by it, is the apparent inability of modern man to spend even the shortest time alone. He anxiously avoids every possibility of self-communion or meditation, as though he feared that reflection might present him with a ghastly self-portrait, such as that of Dorian Gray. The only explanation for the widespread addiction to noise—paradoxical considering how neurasthenic people are today—is that something has to be suppressed. One day, when my wife and I were walking in the woods, we were surprised to hear the rapidly approaching, metallic sounds of a transistor radio. As its owner, a lone, sixteen-year-old cyclist, came into view, my wife remarked, "He's afraid of hearing the birds sing." I think he was only afraid of meeting himself. Why, otherwise, do perfectly intelligent people prefer the inane advertisements on television to their own company? I am sure it is because it helps them to dispel reflection.

People *suffer* from the nervous strain of competition with their fellows. Though trained from earliest youth to see progress in all the mad excesses of competition, those who are the most progressive show most clearly the panic in their eyes, and those who are the most efficient and move fastest "with the times" die an early death from heart attacks.

Even on the unjustifiably optimistic assumption that the earth's population may not continue to increase at its present alarming rate, we must realize that the economic race of man against himself is enough to destroy him completely. Every cycle with a positive feedback leads sooner or later to catastrophe, and the process under discussion contains several cycles of this kind. Besides the commercial, intraspecific selection for an ever faster working pace, there is a second dangerous cycle at work: as described by Vance Packard in several of his books, this process brings in its train a progressive escalation of the *wants* of mankind. For obvious reasons, every producer tries to step up the need of the consumer for the goods manufactured by him. Many "scientific" research institutes are concerned solely with the question of which means are most likely to achieve this reprehensible end. For reasons discussed in Chapters

1 and 8, most consumers are stupid enough to let themselves be steered by methods based on results of opinion polls and advertising research. For example, nobody rebels against the fact that with every tube of toothpaste, with every razor blade, he is forced to buy a package that serves only the ends of advertisement and often costs as much or more than the product itself.

The effects of luxury, produced by the vicious circle of supply-and-demand escalation, will sooner or later be the ruin of the Western world, particularly the United States. Eventually Western peoples will no longer be able to compete with the less pampered and more healthy peoples of the East. It is, therefore, an extremely shortsighted policy of Western capitalists to adhere to their present method of rewarding the consumer by raising his "standard of living," thus "conditioning" him to continue his blood-pressure-raising, nerve-racking race with his neighbor.

In the next chapter, we will deal with still another by-product of luxury, a cycle of destructive phenomena of a very special kind.

Five

Entropy of Feeling

The formation of conditioned reactions is brought about by two kinds of stimuli acting antagonistically; first, by conditioning stimuli strengthening the behavior preceding them (reinforcement), and second, by deconditioning, extinguishing stimuli, weakening or completely inhibiting such behavior. In humans, the action of the first kind of stimuli is associated with feelings of pleasure, those of the second with unpleasurable experience. In higher animals, too, we may describe these, without anthropomorphizing, as reward and punishment.

Why should the phylogenetically evolved program of the organization responsible for this kind of learning work with two and not simply with one kind of stimuli? There are various answers to this question, the most obvious one being that the effectiveness of the conditioning process will be doubled if the organism is enabled to draw expedient consequences not only from success or failure, but from both. There is another hypothetical answer: when the desired effect is to keep the organism away from certain harmful influences and to maintain it at its optimum of warmth, light, humidity, and so on, the action of punishing stimuli will be quite sufficient; we actually see that the appetences for an optimum, that is, for freedom for stimuli, described by Wallace Craig as "aversions," are mostly achieved in this way. If, however, the object is to train the animal to a very specific behavior pattern, even if this is only an activity such as entering a certain, narrowly circumscribed place, it will be difficult to drive it there by stimuli producing solely negative responses. It is easy to drive an animal away from a flower bed but not so easy to drive it into a cage. Wallace Craig has shown that evolution has favored the method of reward wherever it has been necessary to induce an animal to look for very specific stimulus situations, such as those eliciting mating or feeding.

These explanations for the dual principle of reward and punishment are valid, as far as they go. A further function of the pleasure-unpleasurable experience principle, and certainly its most important one, becomes recognizable only when a pathological disorder reveals the consequences of its absence. In the history of medicine and physiology, it has often happened that a physiological mechanism has only manifested its presence by the symptoms of its disease. Every inculcation of a behavior pattern, by a reward strengthening it, causes the organism to endure momentary unpleasurable experience for the sake of pleasure following it or, expressed objectively, to accept, without reaction, stimulus situations which, without the previous conditioning processes, would have an extinguishing, deconditioning effect.

In order to get hold of a tempting prey, a dog or a wolf will do many things that normally he would not do: he will run through thorns, jump into cold water, and expose himself to dangers he would otherwise avoid. The survival function of all these deconditioning mechanisms obviously lies in the fact that they form a counterbalance to the action of the conditioning process. They prevent the animal striving for the rewarding stimulus situation from making sacrifices and taking risks in no proportion to the expected reward. The organism cannot afford a price that "does not pay." A wolf cannot afford to go hunting in the coldest, stormiest night of the polar winter and perhaps pay for a meal with a frozen toe. However, under certain circumstances, it *may* be advisable to take such a risk, for example, if the animal is on the verge of starvation and has to stake all on the last card in order to survive.

That the purpose of the counteraction of reward and punishment, pleasure and unpleasurable experience is to weigh the price with the expected gain, is plainly to be seen by the fact that the intensity of both principles fluctuates according to the economic situation of the organism. When, for example, there is a surfeit of food, its allurement effect sinks so low that the animal will be disinclined to walk even a few steps to get it; the slightest unpleasurable-experience stimulus will suffice to block appetence for food. Conversely, the adaptability of the pleasure-unpleasurable-experience mechanism allows the organism to pay, in an emergency, an exorbitant price for the achievement of a vital end.

The apparatus effecting, in all higher organisms, this

vital adaptation of behavior to the "market situation," possesses certain fundamental physiological properties in common with nearly all neurosensory organizations on the same level of complexity. First, it is subject to the widespread process of sensory adaptation; that is to say, a stimulus combination occurring many times in succession gradually loses its effect, although, and this is essential, there is no change in the threshold value of the reaction to other very similar stimulus situations. Second, the adapting mechanism possesses the likewise widespread property of inertia. For example, when, by the action of strong unpleasurable-experience-eliciting stimuli, balance is displaced, on cessation of these stimuli the system does not return to the normal state of indifference through a mild, "dampened" curve, but it first overshoots this state of quiescence and registers cessation of unpleasurable experience as a marked pleasure. The old joke about the man who persistently hit himself on the head with a hammer because it felt so good when he stopped, here hits the nail on the head.

Both the sensory adaptation and the inertia of the pleasure-unpleasurable experience organization are important to the aims of the treatise. Under the living conditions of modern, civilized man, they can lead to dangerous disturbances of the pleasure-unpleasurable experience economy. Before I discuss these disorders, I must say more about the physiological properties of that economy. They emerged under the ecological conditions prevailing when the mechanisms under discussion—beside many other innate programmings of human behavior—had evolved. At that time, man's life was difficult and dangerous. As a hunter and carnivore, he was at all times dependent on his chances of catching a prey, nearly always hungry, and never sure of his food. As a tropical creature, gradually advancing into more temperate latitudes, he must have suffered greatly from the climate, and since, with his primitive weapons, he was in no way superior to the large predators of his time, he must have lived in a permanent state of anxious alertness.

Under these conditions, much that we look upon today as "sinful," or at least as despicable, was a perfectly appropriate, vital strategy of survival. Overeating was a virtue, for when at last a large animal had been trapped, the most sensible thing a man could do was to eat as much as he possibly could. The same applied, analogously, to the deadly sin of sloth: the effort required to catch a prey was so tremendous that it was advisable, in the interim, to expend no more energy than was absolutely necessary. The dangers besetting man from all sides were so threatening that it was irresponsible to take unnecessary risks, and the utmost caution, bordering on cowardice, was the only sensible maxim of all conduct. In short, at the time when most of the instincts still within us today were programmed, our ancestors had no need to seek difficulties and dangers in a "manly" or heroic way, for these were thrust upon them to an extent only just bearable. Man's phylogenetically evolved pleasure-unpleasurable experience mechanism forced him to avoid all avoidable dangers and all unnecessary expenditure of energy, a principle absolutely expedient at that time.

If, under conditions of modern civilization, the same mechanism produces disastrous malfunctions, this is because of man's phylogenetic construction and the two fundamental physiological properties of sensory adaptation and inertia. In remote antiquity, sages realized that it was not to man's advantage if his striving for pleasure and avoidance of unpleasurable experience met with too much success. In many of the highly civilized societies of the past, people became greatly adept in the avoidance of unpleasurable experience-producing stimulus situations, a state that often led to a dangerous going soft, and even to the fall of a civilization. Very early on, human beings discovered that they could enhance the effect of pleasure-producing situations by sophisticated combinations of stimuli and prevent boredom and blunting of sensation by the play of continuous change. This discovery, made in every higher civilization, leads to *vice*, which, however, is not nearly as culturally destructive as going soft tends to be. As long as men of wisdom have thought and written, these two weaknesses have been denounced, but the greater emphasis has always been on vice.

The development of modern technology and particularly of pharmacology furthers, in unprecedented measure, the general human striving toward unpleasurable-experience avoidance. We no longer fully realize how dependent we have become on modern "comfort," so much do we take it for granted. The most undemanding domestic servant would protest indignantly were she offered a room with the heating and lighting, with the sleeping and washing accommodation that was quite good enough for Madame Pompadour. Even those of us who are most convinced of the advantages of the good old days and of the educational value of the Spartan life, would reconsider our opinion if we had to be operated on by the surgical methods of two hundred years ago.

With progressive control over his environment, modern man has moved the "state of the market" of his pleasure-unpleasurable experience economy in the direction of ever-increasing intolerance of all stimulus situations that produce unpleasurable experience and to an apathy toward all pleasure-eliciting ones. For various reasons, this state of affairs has deleterious effects.

The growing sensitivity to unpleasurable experience —combined with the diminished attractivity of pleasure —has the consequence that people lose the capacity to invest hard work in undertakings that promise pleasure only at some future time. There is, therefore, an impatient demand for *instant gratification* of all budding wishes. Unfortunately, this longing is furthered by a society in which producers push toward consumption; astonishingly enough, consumers do not realize to what extent they are being enslaved by the "accommodating" payment on the instalment-plan system.

For obvious reasons, the compelling desire for instant gratification has particularly deleterious results in sexual behavior. With the loss of the ability to pursue a distant goal, all delicately differentiated behavior patterns of courtship and pair formation disappear. This is true not only of instinctive but also of culturally programmed patterns, that is, not only of those patterns that have evolved in the course of phylogenesis for the purpose of keeping partners together, but also of analogous, specifically human, cultural norms of behavior, such as betrothal and marriage. To describe the consequences of this loss—namely, instant copulation, glorified in so many films today and raised to the level of the norm—as "animal" or "bestial" is quite misleading, for, in higher wild animals, such behavior is extremely rare. It is characteristic only of domestic animals since, in the interests of easy stock breeding, man has "bred out" all highly differentiated behavior patterns of mating.

Since, as we have seen, the mechanism of pleasure-unpleasurable experience economy has the property of inertia and, concomitantly, that of contrast formation, the exaggerated desire to avoid at all costs the least unpleasurable experience has the inevitable result that certain forms of pleasure, dependent on contrast effects, become unattainable. The old saying "Nothing ventured, nothing won" is in danger of being forgotten. With faint-hearted avoidance of unpleasurable experience, joy has become elusive. The psychologist Helmut Schulze has drawn attention to the remarkable fact that the word *Freude* ("joy") does not occur in Freud, who recognizes pleasure but not joy. Schulze says, in substance, that when, sweating and exhausted, with sore fingers and aching limbs, we reach the summit of a difficult mountain, knowing that the even more difficult and dangerous descent lies ahead of us, this is not pleasure but one of the greatest joys on earth. Pleasure may be achieved without paying the price of strenuous effort, but joy cannot. Intolerance of unpleasurable experience converts the natural ups and downs of human life into an artificial plain, the great waves of mountain and valley becoming a scarcely noticeable ripple, and light and shade a monotonous gray. In short, intolerance of unpleasurable experience creates deadly boredom.

This "emotional entropy" seems to threaten particularly those pleasures and pains that are inherent in our *social* ties, ties between married partners and children, between parents, relations, and friends. The conjecture, expressed by Oskar Heinroth in 1910, "that in our behavior toward family and friends, in our courtship and our forming of friendships, purely innate processes are involved that are much more primeval than we think," has been proved absolutely correct by modern ethological research. The genetic programming of all these highly complex behavior patterns entails not only pleasure but also much suffering. The wish to avoid all suffering implies the withdrawal from an essential part of human life. This tendency, in conjunction with the already discussed consequences of overpopulation, the wish "not to get involved," produces a truly alarming syndrome. In certain cultures, the desire to circumvent grief at any cost shows its bizarre and uncanny effects in the reaction to the death of a beloved person. In large sections of the American population, reaction to a death is repressed in the Freudian sense; the deceased has suddenly disappeared, is no longer mentioned; in fact, it would be tactless to do so, and one behaves as though he had never existed. Even more appalling is the dressing up of the dead, portrayed in Evelyn Waugh's cruel satire *The Loved One*. The corpse is "made up" artistically, and it is good manners to admire its attractive appearance.

In comparison with the devastating effects wrought by extreme unpleasurable-experience avoidance on genuine human feelings, the consequences of an equally unrestrained striving for pleasure are almost harmless. One is tempted to say that modern civilized man is too blasé to develop a marked vice. Since the progressive shrinking of the capacity to experience pleasure generally results from adaptation to strong and ever stronger stimulus situations, it is not surprising that blasé people are always seeking *new* stimuli. This "neophilia" applies to nearly all the relations to environmental objects that man is capable of forming. For the man afflicted with this "civilizational" disease, anything he has owned for a certain period loses its attraction, be it a pair of shoes, a suit, a car, or even his friend. Many Americans when moving, will sell without qualm their entire possessions and buy new ones. The advertisements of various travel agencies lure people with the "chance of making new friends." It may seem paradoxical, even cynical to say that the regret we feel when throwing away an old pair of trousers or a faithful old pipe has certain roots in common with our social ties to human friends. When I consider my feelings on selling our old car, bound up in my mind with so many happy journeys, I maintain that these sentiments are qualitatively akin to those experienced when parting from a human friend.

In connection with an inanimate object, this reaction is of course perverse, but when applied to a higher animal, for instance, a dog, it is not only justifiable but can be a test of a person's generosity or meanness of spirit. I have inwardly broken with many people who have said of their dog, "And then we moved into town and had to get rid of him."

"Neophilia" is a phenomenon most welcome to mass producers, and, thanks to the indoctrinability of the masses, of which I will speak in Chapter 8, it can be exploited on the grand scale for commercial profit. "Built-in" obsolescence is an important factor in clothes and car fashions.

In conclusion, let us consider what therapeutic measures might be taken against all this "going soft" and shriveling of feeling. Easy though it may be to understand their causes, it is nonetheless difficult to eliminate them. What has been lost is evidently natural obstacles, the surmounting of which were hardening the individual through the imposition of unpleasurable-experience tolerance as a preliminary to the joy of achievement. The main difficulty lies in the fact that, as I have said, this obstacle must be a "given" one. There is no satisfaction in overcoming purposely created difficulties. The educator Kurt Hahn had great therapeutic success by having blasé, bored young men engaged as lifeguards. In such test situations, which challenge the depth of the personality, many of the young men were cured of their sense of futility. Helmut Schulze, in a similar effort, purposely placed his patients in genuinely threatening "borderline" situations, in which confrontation with the hard facts of reality knocked sense into them. Successful though these therapeutic methods, developed independently by Hahn and Schulze, have been, they provide no general solution to the problem, for we cannot arrange enough shipwrecks to cure all those who have need of their healing effects, nor can we put patients in gliders and so terrify them that they start to realize it is good to be alive. Strangely enough, a model of possible cure may be seen in those not at all exceptional cases, in which the boredom of emotional entropy leads to an attempt at suicide resulting in more or less severe permanent injury. An experienced Viennese teacher of the blind once told me that young people who in a suicide attempt had shot themselves in the head and become blind for life, had never again tried to take their own lives. Not only did they go on living, but they matured into balanced, even happy people. A similar case I know of concerns a woman who, as a girl, had jumped out a window, breaking her back; though paralyzed from the waist down, she later managed to live a happy and contented life. With all these young people, a genuinely challenging obstacle with which they found themselves confronted made life again worth living.

There is no lack of obstacles that have to be overcome if humanity is not to perish, and surmounting them is enough of a challenge to provide every one of us with adequate chances of proving our mettle and merit. It would be a rewarding educational task to make young people aware of these obstacles.

Six

Genetic Decay

There are certain social behavior patterns useful to the community but against the interests of the individual. As Norbert Bischof has recently demonstrated, it is difficult to explain the origin and, more particularly, the retention of these "altruistic" behavior patterns by the principles of mutation and selection. Even though the somewhat inscrutable processes of group selection, which I will not go into here, can explain the origin of "altruistic" behavior patterns, the social system arising in this way by its very nature remains *unstable*. If, for example, in the jackdaw, *Coloeus monedula L.*, a defense reaction has evolved, in which every individual bravely defends a fellow against a predator, it is easy to see that a group with this behavior pattern has better chances of survival than one without it; but what prevents the occurrence, *within* the group, of individuals lacking this comrade-defense reaction? Defective mutations are to be expected and, sooner or later they are almost bound to occur. If they affect this selfless behavior pattern, they must mean a selection advantage for the in-

dividual concerned, provided that the defense of a con-
specific is dangerous. We would therefore expect that
sooner or later such "asocial elements," parasitic on the
social-behavior patterns of the normal society members,
would infiltrate the society. All this obviously applies
only to those socially living animals in which the functions of reproduction and communal labor are not split
up between different individuals, as is the case in "state-
forming" insects. In these, the problems described above
are nonexistent, which is probably the reason why the
altruism of their workers and soldiers has taken on such
extreme forms.

In the case of social vertebrates, we do not know what
has prevented the pervasion of the society by social
parasites. It is certainly difficult to imagine, for example, a jackdaw objecting to the "cowardice" of a social
companion who did not participate in a fellow-defense
reaction. "Objecting" to asocial behavior is known only
on a relatively low, and on the highest, integration level
of living systems, namely, on that of the "cell-state" and
that of the human society. Immunologists have discovered the highly significant fact that there is a close
connection between the capacity to form antibodies and
the danger of malignant-tumor formation. It might even
be supposed that production of specific defense sub-
stances was "invented" only under the selection pressure exerted in long-living and particularly in long-
growing organisms, elicited by the permanent risk that,
in the innumerable cell divisions, dangerous "asocial"
cell forms could arise by defect mutations. Neither

malignant tumors nor antibody formation occur in invertebrates; both arise suddenly in the lowest vertebrates, in cyclostomes such as lampreys, for example. We would probably all die in early youth of malignant tumors had our bodies not produced, in the form of immunity reactions, a kind of "cell police" to deal with asocial elements before they get out of hand.

In human societies the normal member possesses highly specific reaction patterns with which he responds to asocial behavior. The gentlest among us reacts violently if he sees a child mistreated or a woman raped. A comparative examination of the law structure in various cultural groups shows a conformity, even in details, that cannot be explained by intercultural relationships. Goethe says, "Alas, there is never any mention of the sense of justice innate in us." However, the belief in the existence of a natural justice, independent of man-made laws, has apparently been associated, since ancient times, with the idea that this justice is of supernatural divine origin.

By a strange coincidence, on the day I began this chapter, I received a letter from Peter H. Sand, the jurist. I quote: "Modern research into comparative law is increasingly concerned with structure *similarities* between the different law systems of the world (for example, Cornell University recently published a team-project study, the *Common Core of Legal Systems*). For the relatively numerous conformities, three explanations have so far been offered: a metaphysical, natural one (corresponding with the theory of the Vitalists in natural science) ; a historical one (exchange of ideas by diffusion and contact between the various law systems, *i.e.,* imitation of learned behavior) ; and an ecological one (adaptation to environmental conditions, infrastructure, *i.e.,* behavior patterns learned by common experience). Furthermore, in recent times, there is the psychological explanation, with direct reference to Freud, of the common 'sense of justice' arising from childhood experiences (instinct conception!). Above all, there is *Psychoanalytic Jurisprudence* by Professor Albert Ehrenzweig in Berkeley. The essence of this new orientation is the recognition that here the social phenomenon 'justice' is reduced to individual structures, and not vice versa as in the traditional theory of justice. Regrettable, on the other hand, is the permanent accent on *learned* behavior patterns, and the neglect of possible *innate* behavior patterns, in law. After reading your collected papers (in parts, hard going for a lawyer!)I am quite convinced that this mysterious 'sense of justice' (the word itself can be traced far back into the older law theory, but without any explanation) rests largely on typical innate behavior patterns."

I entirely agree with this opinion, though I am fully aware of the difficulties in proving it. Whatever future research may tell us about the phylogenetic and historical sources of man's sense of justice, we may accept it as a scientific fact that the species Homo sapiens has a highly differentiated system of behavior patterns at his disposal, which, in a way analogous to that of the system of antibody formation in the cell state, serves to eliminate socially dangerous elements.

The contemporary criminologist also asks the question: Which parts of criminal behavior rest on genetic defects of innate social behavior patterns and inhibitions, and which parts can be explained by disorders in the cultural transmission of social norms? To arrive at a satisfactory answer to the question is of even greater practical importance than to find the equally difficult juridical solution. Right is right, whether the structure of the law is determined by phylogenetic or by cultural evolution. In judging a criminal, the question whether his defect is of genetic or educational origin is of signal importance when we consider his chances of reintegration into society. This, however, does not imply that genetic aberrations cannot be corrected by purposeful training. In the same way, according to Ernst Kretschmer, many leptosomes can acquire secondarily an almost athletic musculature by means of gymnastics performed with schizothymic consistency. If everything phylogenetically programmed were, *ipso facto*, incapable of being influenced by learning and education, man would be the irresponsible plaything of his instinctive drives. It is the prerequisite of all civilized communal life that people learn to control their impulses: the exhortations of the ascetics stress this very truth. However, the control exercised by reason and responsibility is not unlimited: it is just sufficient to fit a sane and healthy man for his place in civilized society. The mentally sound person and the psychopath differ—to use an old metaphor of mine—no more from each other than a man with a compensated heart defect differs from a man with a decompensated one. As Arnold Gehlen aptly says, man is by nature, *i.e.*, by his phylogenesis, a cultural being. In other words, his instinctive drives and the culturally conditioned, responsible control over them form *one* system, in which the functions of both subsystems are exactly in tune. A slight excess or deficiency on one side or the other leads more easily to disorder than is imagined by all those people who tend to believe in the omnipotence of human reason and learning. Unfortunately, the extent of compensation that a man can achieve by training his control over his impulses is apparently very limited.

Criminology knows all too well how small are the chances of socializing emotionally defective people. This applies to the innately defective as well as to those unfortunates who have acquired a similar disorder by faulty upbringing, for instance, through early hospitalization, as described by René Spitz. Lack of personal contact with the mother during earliest childhood produces—if not still worse effects—the inability to form social ties, with symptoms extremely similar to those of innate emotional deficiency. Certainly not all innate defects are incurable, nor are all acquired ones curable. The old adage "Prevention is better than cure" applies to mental illnesses, too.

The belief in the omnipotence of the conditioned reaction is largely to blame for certain bizarre judicial errors. In his lectures at the Menninger Clinic in Topeka, Kansas, in 1960 Frederick Hacker described the case of a juvenile murderer, admitted to hospital for psychotherapeutic treatment. After a certain period, he was discharged as "cured"; shortly afterward, he committed another murder. This process repeated itself no fewer than four times, and it was only after the criminal had killed his fourth victim, that the humane, democratic, and behavioristic community came to the conclusion that he was a genuine threat to his fellow men.

These four corpses are a minor tragedy in comparison with the damage done by the contemporary attitude toward crime in general: the belief, raised to a doctrine, that all men are born equal and that all moral defects of the criminal are attributable to defects in his environment and education, lead to attrition of the natural sense of justice, particularly in the delinquent himself; filled with self-pity, he regards himself as the victim of society. Recently, the following headline appeared in an Austrian newspaper: FEAR OF HIS PARENTS DRIVES 17-YEAR-OLD YOUTH TO MURDER. The boy had raped his ten-year-old sister and, when she threatened to tell their parents, he strangled her. It is possible that the parents, in a complex chain of effects, may have been partly to blame, but certainly not because they had frightened the boy too much.

These plainly pathological extremes of opinion formation are understandable only if we know that opinion forming is the function of one of those self-regulating systems that tend to *oscillate*. Public opinion is *inert:* It reacts to new influences only after a protracted "dead time"; moreover, it loves gross simplifications, mostly exaggerations of the facts. Therefore, the opposition, criticizing a general opinion, is nearly always in the right; but, in the tug-of-war, it swings to extreme points that it never would have reached had it not tried to counteract the opposing view. Then, if the hitherto prevailing opinion breaks down, as it tends to do quite suddenly, the pendulum swings to the equally exaggerated extreme of what used to be the opposing view.

Our present-day caricature of a liberal democracy has reached the culminating point of an oscillation. At the opposite extreme, reached by the pendulum not long ago, are Eichmann and Auschwitz, "euthanasia," racial hate, massacre, and lynch law. We must realize that, at both sides of the point the pendulum would indicate if it ever stopped moving, there are *genuine values:* on the "left" the value of free, individual development, on the "right" the value of social and cultural soundness. It is the excesses in *both* that lead to inhumanity. The swing of the pendulum becomes increasingly wider; in the United States there are at present dangerous signs that, in reaction to the thoroughly justifiable but excessive rebellion of the young, both white and black, extreme rightist elements are seizing the opportunity to provoke, with stubborn immoderation, the rebound to the other extreme. Worst of all, these ideological oscillations not only run on unchecked but show dangerous signs of escalating to a regular catastrophe. It is up to scientists to find means of *checking* this diabolical oscillation.

It is one of the many dilemmas into which mankind has maneuvered itself that here again, what humane feelings demand for the individual is in opposition to the interests of mankind as a whole. Our sympathy with the asocial defective, whose inferiority might be caused just as well by irreversible injury in early infancy as by hereditary defects, endangers the security of the non-defective. In speaking of human beings, even the words "inferior" or "valuable" cannot be used without arousing the suspicion that one is advocating the gas chamber.

Unquestionably the mysterious "sense of justice" referred to by Peter Sand, rests on a system of genetically anchored reactions, causing us to take action against asocial behavior of fellow human beings. These reactions set the basic theme, unchangeable throughout the ages, around which are composed the systems of justice and morality evolved independently in different cultural groups. Serious malfunctions of this unreflected sense of justice are undoubtedly just as likely to occur as disorders of any other instinctive reaction pattern. The member of an alien cultural group who "does the wrong thing" (for example, the members of the first German New Guinea expedition who felled a sacred palm) will be killed with the same feelings of self-righteousness as those displayed toward a member of a society who has committed, perhaps innocently, a crime against the taboos of that society. "Mobbing," so easily leading to lynch law, is indeed one of the most inhuman behavior patterns to which normal contemporary humans can be driven. It is the root cause of all the cruelties to the "barbarians" outside, as well as to the minorities inside, one's own society. It enhances the tendency to pseudospecies formation, in Erikson's interpretation, and it underlies many other projection phenomena well known to social psychology, for example, seeking a scapegoat for one's own misdeeds, and many other, extremely dangerous and unethical impulses, which, indistinguishable to the intuition of the uninitiated, are absorbed into the universal "sense of justice."

Nevertheless, this sense of justice is as indispensable for the interaction of our social behavior patterns as the thyroid is for our hormones, and the modern tendency to condemn it wholesale and render it ineffective is just as fallacious as were the attempts to cure exophthalmic goiter by total extirpation of the thyroid. The dangerous tendency to eliminate the natural sense of justice by today's absolute tolerance is strengthened by the pseudo-democratic doctrine that all human behavior is learned. Much in our society-sustaining or society-destroying behavior is the blessing or curse of early infantile imprinting by more—or by less—understanding, responsible, and, above all, emotionally sound parents. Just as much, if not more, is genetically fixed. We know that the great regulator, the responsible, categorical imperative, has only a limited power to compensate educational and genetic shortcomings in social behavior. If we have learned to think biologically, and realize the power of instinctive impulses as well as the relative impotence of all conscious morality and good intentions, and if, in addition, we have some psychological and psychiatric insight into the origin of disorder of social behavior, we are unable to condemn the "delinquent" with the self-righteous anger of the naïve person. We see, in the defective, the pitiable invalid rather than the satanic sinner and, purely theoretically, this is perfectly correct. If, however, we combine this justifiable way of thinking with the fallacious view of the pseudo-democratic doctrine, that all human behavior is structured by conditioning and can therefore be changed and corrected to an unlimited extent, we sin against society.

In order to understand the dangers arising from hereditary instinct defects, we must realize that, under conditions of modern, civilized life, there is not a single factor exerting selection pressure in the direction of goodness and kindness, unless it is our innate feeling for these values. Whoever is lacking in this purely emotional sense of values is automatically deaf to all admonitions and sermons. In the commercial competition of Western civilization, there is a plainly negative premium on them! It is fortunate that commercial success is not necessarily positively correlated with reproduction rate.

A good illustration of the value of morality is found in an old Jewish story: a billionaire goes to a marriage broker and tells him he is looking for a wife. The broker enthusiastically sings the praises of a beautiful girl who was Miss America three times running. But the rich man shakes his head. "I am beautiful enough myself!" With the pliancy of his profession, the broker proceeds to extol another prospective bride whose dowry is several million dollars. "I don't need riches. I'm rich enough myself." The broker produces a third file and offers a bride who, at twenty-one, was lecturer in mathematics and now, at twenty-four, is professor of information theory at M.I.T. "I don't need brains," says the billionaire contemptuously. "I'm brainy enough myself!" The broker cries out in desperation, "What, in heaven's name, *do* you want?" "Goodness," is the answer.

We know from our domestic animals, even from wild forms bred in captivity, how quickly social-behavior patterns disintegrate when specific selection is missing. In several fish species, bred for a few generations by commercial dealers, the genetic pattern of brood tending is so disturbed that, among dozens of fishes, one barely finds a pair still capable of caring for their young. As in the deterioration of culturally determined social-behavior norms, here, too, the most highly differentiated and historically youngest mechanisms seem to be particularly susceptible to disorder. The old, ubiquitous drives, such as feeding and pairing, often tend to become hypertrophied. We must, however, consider that man as a breeder selects for indiscriminate, greedy feeding and for the same kind of mating drives; at the same time, he aims to breed out undesirable aggression and flight impulses.

Seen as a whole, the domestic animal is indeed a sad caricature of its owner. In a former work, "Part and Parcel in Animal and Human Societies" (1950), I showed that our aesthetic sense of values is clearly associated with those physical changes that occur in the evolution of the domestic animal: muscular atrophy and fatness, with resultant pot belly, shortening of the base of the skull and the extremities, are typical characteristics of domestication and seem ugly in animal and man, while the opposite characteristics appear "noble." Correspondingly, we value intuitively those behavior characteristics that are destroyed, or at least endangered, by domestication: mother love, self-sacrifice in the interests of family and society are behavior norms just as instinctively programmed as eating and mating, but we regard them unequivocally as better and nobler than these.

In "Part and Parcel in Animal and Human Societies," I described in detail the close relation that exists between the threat to certain characteristics by domestication, and the values set upon them by our ethical and aesthetic sense. The correlation is too evident to be purely coincidental, and the only explanation lies in the inference that our value judgments rest on built-in mechanisms that intercept certain decay phenomena threatening mankind. Similarly, it may be assumed that our sense of justice rests on a phylogenetically programmed apparatus, which prevents the infiltration of society by asocial conspecifics.

A syndrome of hereditary changes, which has undoubtedly arisen in an analogous way and for the same reasons in man and his domestic animals, consists in the remarkable combination of sexual precociousness and persistent youthfulness. Many years ago, L. Bolk showed that man, in many physical characteristics, is much nearer to the adolescent form of his nearest zoological relations than to the adult animals. Arrested development at the stage of youth is known biologically as neoteinia. L. Bolk demonstrates this phenomenon in man, laying particular stress on the retardation of human ontogenesis. What applies to the ontogenesis of the human body, holds good, in a similar way, for that of human behavior. As I have tried to show in "Psychologie und Stammesgeschichte" (1943), man's playful, exploratory curiosity, persisting into old age, his "openness to the world," as Arnold Gehlen in his *Der Mensch* calls it, is a permanent characteristic of youth.

To be childlike is one of the most important, indispensable, and, in the best sense, human characteristics of man. Schiller says, "Man is only wholly man when he plays." "In every real man a child is hidden that wants to play," says Nietzsche. "How do you mean, hidden?" asks my wife. At our first meeting, Otto Hahn, the atomic physicist, said to me, "Tell me, are you a child? I hope you don't misunderstand me!"

Undoubtedly, childlike qualities are among the prerequisites of becoming human. The question is only whether this genetic retardation is not going too far. I have explained (on page 37) how the phenomenon of intolerance of the unpleasurable and emotional attrition can lead to infantile behavior. There is reason to suspect that, in addition to culturally determined processes, genetic changes may be involved. The impatient demand for instant gratification, the lack of any sense of responsibility and consideration for the feelings of others, are typical of little children and, in them, forgivable. The ability to work patiently for a distant goal, a sense of responsibility for one's own behavior, and consideration

for the feelings of others are behavior norms characteristic of the *mature* person.

Cancer-research scientists speak of *immaturity* as one
of the fundamental properties of a malignant growth.
When a cell relinquishes all those properties that make
it a member of a certain body tissue, of the epidermis,
of the intestinal epithelium, or of the mammary gland,
it "regresses" to a state corresponding to a phylogenetically or ontogenetically earlier developmental phase,
i.e., it begins to behave like a unicellular organism or an
embryonic cell, starting to divide without consideration
for the body as a whole. The farther the regression goes,
the more the newly formed tissue diverges from the
normal, and the more malignant is the tumor. Except for
the fact that it protrudes as a wart from the tissue sur-
face, a papilloma still possesses many of the properties
of normal epithelium, and is thus a benign growth; a
sarcoma, consisting of many identical, completely un-
differentiated mesoderm cells is a malignant tumor. As
already implied, the devastating growth of malignant
tumors depends on the fact that certain defensive measures normally protecting the body against asocial cells
fail to act or are rendered impotent by the tumor cells.
It is only when these malignant cells are treated by the
surrounding tissue cells as their own kind and are
nourished by them that the deadly infiltrative growth
sets in.

My earlier analogy (page 44) goes further. A man
whose social-behavior norms have not matured and who
has thus remained in an infantile state, cannot help be-

coming a parasite on society. He takes for granted that he will go on enjoying the adult protection normally only accorded to children. A German newspaper recently reported the case of a young man who killed his grandmother for the sake of a few marks for a movie ticket. He later tried to exonerate himself by stubbornly repeating that he had *told* his grandmother he needed the money for the movies. This young man was, of course, mentally deficient.

Countless young people are hostile to modern society and to their parents. The fact that, in spite of this attitude, they still expect to be kept by this society and their parents shows their unreflecting infantilism.

If the progressive infantilism and the increasing juvenile delinquency are, as I fear, signs of genetic decay, humanity as such is in grave danger. In all probability, our instinctive high valuation of goodness and decency is the only factor today exerting a fairly effective selection pressure against defects of social behavior. Even the hardened moneymaker in our story wants to marry a good girl. Everything discussed in the foregoing chapters—overpopulation, commercial competition, destruction of our natural environment, and alienation from its awe-inspiring harmony, the withering away of the capacity to feel strongly about anything —all these work together to rob man of his ability to distinguish between right and wrong. In addition, there is our exculpation of asocial elements, forced upon us by insight into the genetic and psychological reasons for their shortcomings.

We must learn to combine judicious understanding of the individual with consideration for the rights of the community. The individual, deficient in certain social-behavior patterns and the feelings that go with them, is indeed a sick man deserving our pity, but the deficiency itself is *unmitigated evil*. Not only is it the negation and regression of the process of creation by which animals evolved into man; it is something much more serious, much more sinister. In some mysterious way, disturbance of moral behavior often leads not merely to deficiency of that which we feel to be good and true but to active hostility toward it. It is this phenomenon that makes many religions believe in an adversary of God. When we consider all that has happened and is happening in the world today, it is difficult to argue with those who believe that we are living in the days of anti-Christ.

There is no doubt that through the decay of genetically anchored social behavior we are threatened by the apocalypse in a particularly horrible form. However, even this danger is easier to avert than others, for instance, overpopulation or the vicious circle of commercial competition, which can be counteracted only by radical measures such as a revaluation of all the pseudo-values worshiped today. To prevent the genetic decline and fall of mankind, all we need do is follow the advice implied in the old Jewish story I quoted earlier. When you look for a wife or husband, do not forget the simple and obvious requirement: she must be *good*, and he no less.

Before going on to the next chapter, which deals with the dangers inherent in the loss of tradition brought about by the all too radical rebellion of the young, I must preclude a possible misunderstanding: all that I have just said about the dangerous consequences of progressive infantilism, particularly about the atrophy of the sense of responsibility and of values, applies to rapidly spreading juvenile criminality but not to the world-wide rebellion of modern youth. However fiercely I may denounce the mistakes they make, I must state just as categorically that these young people certainly do not suffer from lack of social and moral sense. On the contrary, they have a very healthy realization not only that something is rotten in the state of Denmark but that a good deal is rotten in considerably greater states.

Seven

The Break
with Tradition

The evolution of a human culture shows several remarkable analogies to the phyletic evolution of species. The *cumulative tradition* at the root of all culture evolution rests on essentially new achievements, unknown in the animal world, for example, conceptual thought and syntactic language, which, by their capacity to form free symbols, open to mankind a hitherto nonexistent possibility of spreading and transmitting individually acquired knowledge. Because of this "inheritance of acquired characteristics," historical development of a culture proceeds much faster than phylogenesis of a species.

The processes by which a civilization acquires and retains new, system-preserving knowledge are different from the processes of species variation; but the method by which the knowledge to be retained is chosen from among the many possibilities offered is apparently the same in the development of species and of cultures, namely, by selection after thorough trial. However, since man, by his ever-increasing domination of nature, eliminates one selection factor after the other, the selection influencing the structures and functions of a culture is not quite so inflexible as that determining species variation. Therefore, in civilizations, we often find something that hardly ever occurs in species: so-called luxury forms, *i.e.*, structures whose form is *not* caused by the selection pressure of a system-preserving function, not even by one that was active in the past. Man can afford to carry around more useless ballast than any wild animal.

Remarkably, it is apparently selection *alone* that decides what is to be assimilated into the permanent knowledge fund of a civilization as traditional, "sacred" customs and habits. It seems also that inventions and discoveries, arrived at by insight and rational exploration, assume a ritual, even religious character, if they have been transmitted long enough. I will come back to this in the next chapter. If we examine the customary social norms of a civilization, as they are at the moment, without submitting them to historical comparisons, we cannot differentiate between those arising from a chance "superstition" and those owing their origin to genuine insight and invention. We might even say that *everything* transmitted over longer periods by cultural tradition finally assumes the nature of a "superstition" or a "doctrine".

At first, this may appear to be a "constructional error" of the mechanism acquiring and storing knowledge in human cultures. However, on further consideration, we find that extreme conservatism in retaining what has once been successfully tried is a vital property of the apparatus performing, in cultural evolution, a task analogous to that of the genes in species variation. Retention is not only equally important; indeed, it is even more important than additional acquisition; and we must realize that without very special investigation we cannot know which customs and usages, transmitted to us by the tradition of our culture, are dispensable, obsolete superstition and which are indispensable, cultural heritage. Even in the case of behavior norms whose bad effects are apparent, such as head-hunting in several tribes of Borneo and New Guinea, we cannot foresee what repercussions their eradication will have on the system of social-behavior norms holding the particular culture group together. In a measure, a system of this kind represents the skeleton of the culture concerned, and, without insight into the multiplicity of its interactions, it is extremely risky to remove arbitrarily one of its elements.

The erroneous belief that only the rationally comprehensible or the scientifically provable belong to the fixed knowledge of mankind produces disastrous effects. It encourages "scientifically enlightened" youth to throw overboard the enormous fund of knowledge and wisdom contained in the traditions of every old civilization and in the teaching of the great world religions. Anyone who believes that all this is null and void is harboring another illusion, just as disastrous, namely, that science can create, from nothing and by reason alone, a whole culture with everything pertaining to it. This notion is only slightly less stupid than the opinion that our knowledge can "better" mankind by interference with the human genes. In a culture, knowledge has "grown" by selection in just the same way as it develops in an animal species, and this, as is well known, we have never been able to "make."

The enormous underestimation of our nonrational, cultural fund of knowledge and the equal overestimation of all that man, as Homo faber, is able to produce by means of his intellect, are not the only factors threatening our civilization with destruction; they are not even the decisive ones. Being enlightened is no reason for confronting transmitted tradition with hostile arrogance and for treating it as a biologist might an old farmer's wife who informs him that fleas are produced by wetting sawdust with urine. The attitude of many of the younger generation toward their parents shows a good measure of conceited contempt but no understanding. The revolt of modern youth is founded on *hatred,* a hatred closely related to an emotion that is most dangerous and difficult to overcome: *national hatred.* In other words, today's rebellious youth reacts to the older generation in the same way that a culture group or "ethnic" group reacts to a foreign, hostile one.

It was Erik Erikson who first pointed out how far-reaching are the analogies between the divergent development of independent ethnic groups in cultural history and the divergent evolution of subspecies, species, and genera. He spoke of "pseudospeciation," of a simulation of species formation. Historically developed rites and norms of social behavior represent the factors that, on the one hand, keep smaller and larger cultural units integrated but, on the other hand, also keep them separate. A certain kind of "manners," a special group dialect, a way of dressing, and so on, can become the symbol of a community that is supported by all its members much in the same way as a group of personally known and cherished friends. As I described in an earlier paper, "Die instinktiven Grundlagen menschlicher Kultur" (1967), this high estimation of all symbols of one's own group goes hand in hand with a corresponding devaluation of the symbols of every other comparable cultural unit. The longer two ethnic groups have developed independently of each other, the greater the differences become. From their similarities and dissimilarities, we can reconstruct the process of their evolution, just as, analogously, we can do this from the differences in characteristics of animal species. In both cases, we can safely assume that the more widespread characteristics, those distributed over greater units, are the older ones.

Any clearly differentiated cultural group tends to consider itself a species apart, insofar as it does not accept the members of other, comparable units as of equal worth. In many native languages the term for one's own tribe is simply "man." To kill a member of a neighboring tribe therefore does not amount to real murder. This consequence of pseudospeciation is extremely dangerous: inhibition against killing a fellow human is largely overcome, while intraspecific aggression, elicited by conspecifics and only by these, remains active. We hate the "enemy" with a hatred reserved only for fellow human beings and not even the most dangerous beast of prey; we can kill them with impunity since we do not feel that they are really human. Naturally it belongs to the well-tried technique of all warmongers to support this view.

It is a disturbing thought that today's younger generation is beginning to treat the older one as an alien pseudospecies. This can be recognized by many symptoms. Competitive and hostile ethnic groups are apt to evolve distinctive national costumes. In Central Europe, local peasant costume has largely died out. Only in those parts of Hungary where Hungarian and Slovak villages are close together has it been preserved. Here the costume is worn proudly and with the obvious intention of provoking members of other ethnic groups. Many self-constituted groups of rebellious youths do precisely the same thing, and it is amazing how—in spite of their ostensible rejection of everything military—the habit of wearing uniforms has become firmly established. The various subgroups, beatniks, hippies, Teddy boys, Rocks, Mods, Rockers, and so on, are, to the "initiated," just as easily recognizable by their uniforms as were the regiments of the Imperial Austrian army.

In customs and usages the rebellious young try to keep as far as possible from the parent generation, not simply by ignoring their forms of behavior but by observing every detail of it and then converting it to the exact opposite. This is one of the explanations for the sexual excesses in people who otherwise seem to have a lowered general sexual potency. Similarly, the intense wish to break through all parental vetoes is the only explanation for the fact that rebelling students have publicly urinated and defecated, as they once did at the University of Vienna. This indicates "regression" to the pretoilet-training phase of early childhood.

The young people concerned are quite unaware of the motivation for all these strange, bizarre behavior patterns, and they give numerous seemingly rational explanations for their behavior. They protest against their parents' indifference with regard to the poor and the hungry, against the war in Vietnam, against the despotism of the university senate, against all establishments of any kind—though remarkably seldom against the rape of Czechoslovakia by the Soviet Union. Actually, however, the attack is directed randomly against all older people, irrespective of their political affiliation. Students of the extreme left attack professors of the extreme left almost as frequently as those of the extreme right. Under the leadership of Daniel Cohn-Bendit, Communist students once vehemently abused Herbert Marcuse, making the most absurd allegations, for instance, that he was on the payroll of the CIA. The demonstrators manifestly were not motivated by the fact that he belonged to another political affiliation but rather by the generation gap.

In the same subconscious and intuitive way, the older generation *understands* what these ostensible protests really are: insults and aggressivity fueled by hatred. And so follows a rapid and dangerous escalation of a hate essentially akin to that between different ethnic groups, in other words, to national hate. Though I am an ethologist, I find it hard not to react angrily to the smart blue tunic of the well-to-do Communist, Cohn-Bendit. The look on the faces of such young people is enough to tell us that this is just what they want. All this reduces to a minimum the prospect of mutual understanding.

In my book *On Aggression* (1963), and in public lectures (1968, 1969), I have discussed the ethological causes of the war between generations. I will therefore limit myself here to the salient points. The whole crisis is based on a functional disorder of the development taking place in man during puberty. During this phase, the young person begins to detach himself from the traditions of his parents, to test them critically and to look around for new ideals and for a new group whose principles he can make his own. The instinctive wish to *fight* for a good cause influences this choice, especially in the case of young men. In this phase, old traditions seem uninteresting and everything new attractive. We might speak of a physiological neophilia.

This process unquestionably has a high system-preserving value and has therefore been absorbed into the phylogenetically evolved program of human behavior. Its function is to lend adaptability to the otherwise too rigid transmission of cultural behavior norms; in this, it is comparable to the molting of a crab which, in order to grow, has to shed its rigid external skeleton. As in all fixed structures, in cultural transmission, too, the indispensable, supporting function must be bought by loss of degrees of freedom; the dismantling necessary in every constructional change brings with it certain dangers, for, between pulling down and building up, there is necessarily a period of instability and defenselessness. This is the case both in the newly molted crab and in the pubescent human.

Normally, the period of physiological neophilia is followed by a revival of love of tradition; this may proceed very gradually, and most of us older ones can testify that, at sixty, we have a much higher opinion of many views held by our fathers than at eighteen. The psychologist Alexander Mitscherlich called this phenomenon "late obedience." Physiological neophilia and late obedience together form a system whose system-preserving function is the elimination of obsolete elements hindering new development, and the preservation of the essential, indispensable structure. Since the structure of this system is necessarily dependent on a great many external and internal factors, it is, understandably, easy to upset.

According to the stage at which it occurs, arrested development caused by environmental or by genetic factors may have very different consequences. To remain arrested at the stage of early infancy may result in fixation on the parents and obstinate adherence to the traditions of the older generation. Such people have little contact with their contemporaries and often become outsiders. Physiologically unwarranted persistence in the stage of neophilia leads to characteristic vindictive resentment toward long-dead parents and, at the same time, to a certain peculiarity of behavior. Both phenomena are well known to the psychoanalyst.

However, the disorders leading to hate and war between the generations have other, twofold causes; first, the necessary adaptive changes in the ever-increasing fund of culture transmitted from generation to generation. In Abraham's time, the necessary alterations in the behavior norms taken over from the father by the son were so imperceptibly small that—as Thomas Mann describes in his remarkable psychological novel *Joseph and His Brethren*—many people of that era found it impossible to differentiate their own personality from that of their father, a condition representing the most perfect form of identification imaginable. The rate of development forced upon today's culture by technology has the result that a considerable part of the traditions still observed by one generation is regarded, rightly, by critical youth as obsolete. The already discussed misconception that man can create a new culture arbitrarily and rationally from nothing leads to the utterly insane idea that it is best to eradicate all parental culture entirely in order to be able to rebuild "constructively." In actual fact, we could do this only by starting afresh at the stage of pre-Cro-Magnon man!

There are, however, still other reasons for the endeavor of modern youth to eradicate parental culture. In the course of our progressive technology, the structure of the family undergoes many changes, all working together to loosen the bonds between parents and children. This starts at the infant stage. The modern mother can hardly ever give her full time to her baby and this results, to a greater or lesser degree, in the phenomenon called, by René Spitz, hospitalization. Its worst symptom is a severe, irreversible lessening of the ability to make human contacts. All this contributes in a serious way to the decay of human compassion that I discussed earlier. At a somewhat later age, particularly in boys, lack of the paternal ideal makes itself felt. Except among farmers and craftsmen, a boy almost never sees his father at work, nor does he have the opportunity of assisting him and coming to appreciate the father's superiority. The contemporary "nuclear" family lacks the rank-order structure that, under more natural conditions, made an old man a venerable figure. Though a five-year-old cannot assess the superiority of his forty-year-old father, he will be impressed by the strength of a ten-year-old, and understand the respect of this boy for his fifteen-year-old brother. Instinctively he draws the right conclusions when he notices how the fifteen-year-old, clever enough to recognize the mental superiority of his father, looks up to him.

Recognition of superiority in rank order is not incompatible with affection. Everybody can remember how, as a child, he loved the people whom he admired and respected, not less but more than he loved his equals or subordinates. I clearly remember how I felt not only respect, and the wish to gain his approbation for acts of bravery, but also deep affection for my late friend, Emanuel la Roche who, four years older than I, reigned as the uncontested leader, justly but strictly, over our wild band of ten-to-sixteen-year-old children. This feeling undoubtedly matched in quality what I felt toward revered older friends and teachers. It is one of the greatest crimes of the pseudodemocratic doctrine that it regards the natural rank order between two people as a frustrating impediment to all warmer feelings. Without such a rank order, not even the most natural form of human love that normally unites the members of a family can develop; thousands of children have become unhappy neurotics because of the well-known "nonfrustration" upbringing.

As I have already explained in the above-mentioned works, a child in a group without rank order finds itself in a thoroughly unnatural situation. Since he cannot suppress his own instinctively programmed striving for higher rank order, he tyrannizes his parents and finds himself in the role of group leader, a position in which he cannot possibly feel satisfied. Without a stronger "superior," he feels unprotected in a hostile world, for nonfrustration children are never popular. When, in understandable irritation, such a child provokes his parents, "begging for a smack," it does not meet the instinctively expected and subconsciously hoped-for counteraggression, but comes up against the padded wall of calm, pseudorational phrases.

Nobody ever identifies with a slavish weakling or allows such a person to dictate behavior norms to him. Still less will anybody accept the cultural values of a person of this kind. Only when we feel deep affection and, at the same time, respect for somebody, are we capable of making his cultural traditions our own. Far too great a majority of modern adolescents lack such a "father figure." Their own father all too often fails in his task and, in the mass organization of schools and universities, his place cannot be filled by an honored preceptor.

In addition to these purely ethological reasons for rejecting parental culture, there are, in the case of many intelligent young people, genuinely ethical ones. In our present-day Western civilization, with its mass organization, its devastation of nature, its value-blind, money-grabbing race against itself, its terrifying loss of feeling, and the stultifying influence of its indoctrination, all that is unworthy of imitation has become so predominant that it tends to obscure the deep truth and wisdom still inherent in our culture. The youth of today *has* indeed cogent reasons for attacking all "establishments." It is, however, difficult to assess what proportion of the rebels, including students, is really acting on these principles. What actually happens in public riots is obviously motivated by other subconscious, ethological impulses, the first of these being, undoubtedly, ethnic hatred. Those young people who are truly reflective and who act from rational motives, are the less violent ones; therefore, the external picture of the rebellion is, unfortunately, dominated by the symptoms of neurotic regression. Due to misplaced loyalty, the reasonable young people are evidently not capable of keeping their distance from the purely impulsive ones.

In discussions with students, I have gained the impression that the proportion of reasonable ones is not as small as would appear at first sight.

However, in reviewing the situation, we must not forget that reasonable considerations are a much weaker motivation than the elementary, instinctive, primitive force of the aggression actually behind them. Still less should we forget the consequences to the young people themselves of the complete rejection of parental tradition. These consequences can be devastating. During the phase of "physiological neophilia," the adolescent is obsessed by an overwhelming desire to join a peer group and, above all, to participate in its collective aggression. This urge is as strong as any other phylogenetically programmed impulse, as strong as hunger and sexuality. As in sexuality, it can, by insight and learning processes, at best become fixed on a certain object, but it can never be completely governed and still less suppressed by reason. Where this apparently succeeds, there is the danger of a neurosis.

In this ontogenetic stage, the "normal" procedure, *i.e.*, that which best serves the system survival of a culture, is for young people of a peer group to get together in the service of new ideals, bringing about the corresponding, essential reforms of the traditional behavior norms without, however, throwing the whole fund of parental culture overboard. Thus the young person identifies himself with a young branch of an old culture. In his deepest essence, man is by nature a cultural being and can therefore find a completely satisfying identification only in and with a culture. When this is denied him, he satisfies his urge for identification and group membership by the same methods used to discharge other unsatisfied instincts, for instance, the sexual drive: he vents it on a *substitute object*. The indiscriminateness with which dammed-up drives are discharged on amazingly unsuitable objects has long been known to science, but there is hardly a more impressive example of it than the object choice frequently made by young people yearning to belong to a group. Any group is better than none, even if this means joining the most tragic of all communities, that of the drug addicts. Aristide Esser, a psychiatrist, and an expert in this field, was able to show that, besides boredom, with which I have already dealt in Chapter 5, the desire to belong to a group drives a steadily increasing number of young people to drugs.

Where there is no group to belong to, there is always the possibility of making one "to measure." Partly or wholly criminal gangs of youths as, for example, in the musical *West Side Story*, represent in schematic simplicity the phylogenetic program of the ethnic group, but one sadly lacking in the traditional culture of a nonpathological community. As shown in this musical, two gangs often form simultaneously, with no other aim than to be the objects for each other's collective aggression. The English Mods and Rockers, if they still exist, are another typical example. These mutually aggressive countergroups are, however, more tolerable than, for example, the Hamburg Rockers who have made it their life's aim to beat up defenseless old people.

Emotional excitement inhibits rational function; the

hypothalamus blocks the cortex. To no other emotion does this apply so strongly as to collective, ethnic hate, all too well known as national hatred. We must realize that the hate of the younger generation for the older stems from the same sources. The workings of hate are worse than total blindness or deafness, for hatred falsifies facts and distorts them. All advice given to rebellious young people, to prevent them from destroying their own most valuable heritage, will predictably be misinterpreted as the underhanded attempt to support the hated "establishment." Hate makes people not only blind and deaf but incredibly stupid. It is going to be difficult to convince them that all that has arisen in cultural evolution is just as indispensable and admirable as that which has evolved in phylogenesis; and it is going to be difficult to convince them that a culture can be snuffed out like a candle.

Eight

Indoctrinability

Oskar Heinroth, archscientist and archridiculer of philosophy, used to say, "What we think is mostly wrong, but what we know is right." This epistemologically unprejudiced sentence expresses perfectly the evolutionary process of all human knowledge, perhaps of knowledge in general. First, we "think something"; then we compare it with experience and with additional sensory data until, from its conformity or nonconformity with these, we conclude the rightness or wrongness of what we have thought. This comparison of an internal conclusion, evolved somehow within the organism, with a second law prevailing in the outside world, is probably the most important method by which a living organism acquires knowledge. Karl Popper and Donald Campbell called this "pattern matching."

In its simplest manifestation, on the lowest level of life processes, this cognitive process takes place principally in the same way; in the physiology of perception it is to be found everywhere, and in the conscious thinking of man it takes the form of conjecture and subsequent confirmation. A great many of our conjectures are proved, by testing, to be wrong, but if one has stood up to testing often enough, we "know" it. In science, these processes are called hypothesis formation and verification.

Unfortunately, these two steps to knowledge are not as sharply differentiated, and the result of the second is in no way as clear as Oskar Heinroth's statement would make it seem. In the edifice of knowledge, the hypothesis is a scaffolding, of which the builder knows in advance that in the execution of his plans he will pull it down. It is a *provisional* assumption, the making of which has sense only if there is the practical possibility of disproving it by facts sought specially for this purpose. A hypothesis inaccessible to "falsification" is not verifiable and is thus useless for experimental work. The constructor of a hypothesis has to be grateful to whoever shows him new ways by which he can prove his hypothesis to be inadequate, for all verification can consist only in demonstrating that the hypothesis resists attempts at disproof. The *work* of every scientist consists essentially in the search for such tests. Thus we speak of working hypotheses, which are the more fruitful the more scope they give for test work: the probabilty of the correctness of such a hypothesis rises with the number of facts brought forward that fit into it.

Among epistemologists, there is widespread belief that a hypothesis is definitively refuted if one or several facts do not fit into it. Were this the case, all existing hypotheses would be refuted, for there is scarcely one that does justice to *all* the relevant facts. All our knowledge is only an *approach* to the extrasubjective reality that we are trying to know. However, it is a progressive approach. A hypothesis is never disproved by a single contradictory fact but only by another hypothesis that can fit in more facts than it can itself. "Truth" is thus the working hypothesis most suitable to pave the way to that other hypothesis which is able to explain more.

However, our thinking and feeling are unable to accept this theoretically indisputable fact. Though we realize that all our knowledge, all the information about the outside world transmitted to us by our perception, represents a highly simplified picture only roughly approaching the thing existing in itself, we cannot prevent ourselves from accepting certain things as true and believing in the absolute rightness of this knowledge.

Considered psychologically and, above all, phenomenologically, this conviction is equatable with a *creed*. When the scientist has verified a hypothesis to the degree that it has earned the name of a theory, and when this theory has proved itself to the degree that it will predictably be altered only by subsidiary hypotheses, and not fundamentally, we "believe" in it "firmly." This belief does no harm, for such a "finished" theory, within its range of validity, still retains its "truth," even if this should be found to be less all-embracing than was thought at the time the theory was propounded. This applies, for example, to all classical physics which, by the quantum theory, was limited in its range of validity but not refuted in the true sense.

In the same way that I accept the theses of classical

mechanics, I "believe" in a whole series of theories that are probable up to the borders of certainty. For example, I am quite convinced that the so-called Copernican world picture is right; at least, I should be extremely surprised if the notorious hollow-world theory should turn out to be true, or if, as people believed at the time of Ptolemy, the planets crawl about the celestial sphere in strange, epicyclic loops.

However, I believe in certain things just as firmly as in proved theories, though I have not the slightest proof that my conviction is right. For example, I believe that the universe is governed by a single set of natural laws, which are free from internal contradictions and which are never transgressed. This conviction, which, for me, is positively axiomatic, excludes extranatural happenings. In other words, I regard all the phenomena described by parapsychologists and spiritualists as self-delusory. This opinion is completely unscientific. Extranatural processes might occur, very rarely and in very slight measure, and the fact that I have never witnessed any that convinced me does not justify any assertion of mine that they do or do not exist. It is, admittedly, my purely religious belief that there is only *one* great miracle, and no miracles, in the plural, or, as the poet-philosopher Kurt Lasswitz has expressed it, that God has no need to perform miracles.

I have said that these convictions—both the scientifically founded and the intuitive—phenomenologically speaking, amount to a creed. In order to give his quest for knowledge an even apparently firm foundation, man cannot do otherwise than accept certain facts as indisputable and base his conclusions on them. In forming a hypothesis, we consciously *feign* the certainty of such a foundation; we "act as though" it were true just to see what comes of it. The longer we have built on such fictitious points, without our building becoming self-contradictory and collapsing, the more probable, according to the principle of mutual elucidation, will be the originally daring assumption that the basic points underlying our hypothesis are real.

The hypothetical inference that certain things simply are *true* belongs to the indispensable processes of human striving for knowledge. It also belongs to the motivational prerequisites of research that we *hope* the assumption to be true, the hypothesis to be correct. There are relatively few scientists who prefer to work by the process of elimination; they exclude experimentally one explanation after the other until the only one remaining is bound to contain the truth. Most of us—and we must realize this—*love* our hypotheses. As I once said, it is a very painful but, at the same time, a healthy and rejuvenating daily morning exercise to throw a pet hypothesis overboard. Naturally, our "love" of hypothesis is influenced also by the length of time we have held it; ways of thinking are habits like any other, and they become so particularly when we have not formed them ourselves but have taken them over from a great and honored teacher. If he was the discoverer of a new explanatory principle and therefore has *many* followers, our adherence will be strengthened by the mass effect of an opinion shared by many people.

There is nothing wrong with these phenomena in

themselves; indeed, they have their justification. A good working hypothesis does actually gain in probability if, in many years of research, no contradictory facts have come to light. The principle of mutual elucidation gains effectiveness as time passes. In addition, it is justifiable to take very seriously the words of a responsible teacher, since he will rigorously examine everything he imparts to his students, and, if necessary, heavily stress the hypothetical nature of his teaching. Such a teacher will consider his theories very thoroughly before he regards them as "fit for a textbook." It is also by no means always reprehensible to feel confirmed in an opinion by the fact that others share it. Four eyes see better than two, and this is all the more true if a fellow scientist, starting from different induction bases, arrives at identical results, since this implies unequivocal corroboration.

Unfortunately, all these factors that confirm or strengthen a conviction may be present unjustifiably. As already mentioned, a hypothesis may have been constructed in such a way that the experiments dictated by it are bound from the first to confirm it. For instance, the hypothesis that the reflex is the only elementary function of the central nervous system worth investigating led solely to those experiments which registered the response of the system to a *change* in condition. These experiments were planned in a manner that precluded their revealing that the central nervous system can do more than react passively to stimuli. We need both self-criticism and imaginative thought if we are to avoid a mistake that devalues the hypothesis, however "fertile" it may be in producing "information" in the sense of the information theory. If we make such a mistake, the hypothesis will cease to lead to further insight or will do so only exceptionally.

Similarly, faith in the teaching of the master, valuable though it may be in the founding of a "school," that is, a new direction of research, incurs the dangers of doctrine formation. The genius who has discovered a new explanatory principle tends, as we know by experience, to overestimate its range of validity. Jacques Loeb, Ivan Petrovich Pavlov, Sigmund Freud and many of the greatest scientists have done this. Moreover, if the theory is all too flexible and therefore offers little incentive to falsification, this, combined with reverence for the master, may turn the pupils into disciples and the school into a religion and a cult, as has happened in various places with the teaching of Sigmund Freud.

The decisive step in the formation of a doctrine, in the narrower sense of the term, is taken, however, when, to the two already discussed supporting forces of a theory an all-too-large *number* of supporters is added. The facility of spreading such a teaching through modern mass media may easily lead to the establishment of a concept that is no more than an unverified scientific hypothesis, swaying not just scientific but public opinion as well.

From there on, unhappily, all those mechanisms come into action which normally serve the preservation of proved traditions, and which we have treated in Chapter 7. People now fight for their doctrinal belief with a vehemence that would be justified only in the defense of the well-proved wisdom and knowledge of an old culture. Anyone who does not conform to the new opinion is branded as a heretic, slandered and, as much as possible, discredited. The highly specialized reaction of "mobbing," of social hate, is directed against him.

Such a doctrine, elevated to an all-embracing religion, gives its supporters the subjective satisfaction of secure knowledge bearing the stamp of revelation. All facts contradicting it are denied, ignored or, more frequently, *repressed,* in the Freudian sense, thrust into the subconscious. The repressor meets every attempt to bring the repressed back to consciousness with an embittered, emotionally charged resistance, which is the stronger, the greater the change required in his opinion, above all, in the opinion he has formed of himself. "Whenever men with conflicting myths encountered one another," says Philip Wylie, in *The Magic Animal,* "there occurred on both sides a repugnance, a sense of error in the other, now seen as the heathen, the infidel, the territorial brigand.

"And holy war began."

All this is by no means new. Goethe says, "In all the Devil's celebrations the most potent ingredient will always be party strife." But indoctrination begins to have satanic effects only when it unites vast human conglomerates, whole continents, even the whole of humanity in a single, or erroneous, evil creed. This very danger is threatening us now. When, at the end of the last century, Wilhelm Wundt made the first serious attempt to turn psychology into a science, strangely enough the new science failed to develop along the lines of biology. Although Darwin's teaching was common property by then, although comparative methods and phylogenetic investigation were established procedures in all other life sciences, they were persistently ignored by the new experimental psychology. It followed strictly the example of physics where, at that time, the atomic theory was paramount. The new psychology assumed that the behavior of living creatures, like all things material, must consist of independent, indivisible elements. At that time, it was natural to regard the reflex as the basic element of behavior. The endeavor, perfectly legitimate, to examine physiological and psychological structures and procedures simultaneously led scientists to correlate the physiological process of conditioning, discovered by I. P. Pavlov, with the psychological processes of association examined by Wundt. It is the prerogative of genius to overestimate the applicability of newly discovered explanatory principles, and thus it is not surprising that these truly epoch-making and convincingly compatible discoveries induced not only their discoverers but also the entire scientific world to believe that "all" animal and human behavior could be explained on the basis of the reflex and the conditioned reflex.

The reflex doctrine and the correlated investigation of the conditioned reflex legitimately met with an enormous initial success; the simplicity of the hypothesis and the apparent exactitude of the experiments led both lines of research to a truly and universally dominant position. However, their great influence on public opinion has still another explanation. When applied to man, these theories solve all the difficulties arising from the existence of the instinctive and the unconscious. The orthodox supporters of the conditioned-reflex doctrine maintain that a human being is born as a completely blank page (Locke's *tabula rasa*), and that all he thinks, feels, knows, and believes is the result of his "conditioning."

For reasons clearly recognized by Philip Wylie, this doctrine found general acclamation. Even religious believers could be converted to it, for if the child is born as a *tabula rasa*, it is the duty of every believer to see to it that this child and, possibly, all other children, are brought up in what he believes to be the only true religion. Thus behavioristic dogma supports every doctrinaire in his conviction, but does nothing to reconcile religious doctrines with each other. Liberal and intellectual Americans, attracted to a sound, simple, easily intelligible and, above all, mechanistic teaching, accepted it almost without exception, particularly because here was a doctrine proclaiming itself as a liberating and democratic principle.

It is an indisputable ethical truth that all men have an equal right to the same chances of development, but this truth is all too easily converted to the untruth that all men are potentially equal. The behavioristic doctrine goes a step further in maintaining that all men would be equal if they could develop under the same external conditions, and indeed that they would become ideal people if only those conditions were ideal. Therefore, people cannot, or *must not*, possess any inherited properties, particularly those that determine their social behavior and their social requirements.

The present-day rulers of America, China, and the Soviet Union are unanimous in one opinion: that unlimited conditionality of man is highly desirable. Their belief in the pseudodemocratic doctrine is—as Wylie maintains—based on the wish that it were true, for these manipulators are certainly not satanically clever supermen but are themselves all-too-human victims of their own inhuman doctrine. It is no exaggeration to call this doctrine inhuman, since everything specifically human is unwelcome to its supporters, who understandably regard as highly desirable all the aforementioned processes of dehumanization that facilitate the manipulation of mankind. "Down with individuality!" is the slogan. It is equally important to the capitalist mass producer as to the Soviet functionary to condition people into uniform, unresisting subjects, not very different from those described by Aldous Huxley in his terrifying novel *Brave New World*.

The fallacy of supposing that, given the proper conditioning, anything may be demanded of a person, anything made out of him, underlies many of the deadly sins committed by civilized mankind against nature, including the nature of man, and against humanity. If a universally accepted ideology, and the politics ensuing from it, are founded on a lie, this is bound to have disastrous effects. The pseudodemocratic doctrine here under discussion undoubtedly bears a considerable part of the blame for the moral and cultural collapse that threatens the Western world.

Alexander Mitscherlich, the psychologist and sociologist, who otherwise is acutely aware of the threat to humanity by indoctrination with a code of fictitious values, has written, to my surprise: "We must not imagine that people today are more obstructed in their individual realization by a sophisticated system of manipulations than they were in the past." I am perfectly convinced that they are. Never were such large human masses divided among so few ethnic groups; never was mass suggestion so effective; never before have the manipulators had at their disposal such clever advertising techniques or such impressive mass media as today.

Considering the fundamental similarity of the aims, it is hardly surprising that the methods by which the various "establishments" try to make their subjects into ideal representatives of the American way of life, into ideal functionaries of the Soviet Union, or into any other ideal kind of people are substantially the same throughout the world.

We ostensibly free, Western, civilized people are no longer conscious of the extent to which we are being manipulated by the commercial decisions of the mass producers. If we travel in the East German Republic or in the Soviet Union, we are struck by the red signs and posters, insidiously suggestive and psychologically effective, reminiscent of Aldous Huxley's babbling ma-

chines, murmuring their propaganda urgently and in-
cessantly. On the other hand, in these countries we are
favorably impressed by the absence of neon signs and
of all wastage. Nothing still useful is thrown away:
newspaper serves to pack purchased goods, and ancient cars are looked after lovingly. Then we gradually
realize that the large-scale advertising of our Western
producers is not unpolitical in nature, but that, in its
own way, it fulfills the same function as posters in
Eastern Europe. Opinions may differ about whether all
that the red signs propagate is bad and stupid, but the
method of discarding scarcely used goods for the purpose
of acquiring new ones, the avalanchelike growth of production and consumption is, demonstrably, as stupid as
it is bad, in the ethical sense of this word. As custom
work and handcrafts are destroyed by the competition
of industry, and small businesses and small farmers are
eliminated, we are all forced to conform to the dictates
of mass manufacturers, to eat the food and wear the
clothes prescribed by them. Worse still, as a result of
our conditioning, we do not even notice that we are
being manipulated.

The most effective way of manipulating great human
masses is to unify their demands by fashion. Originally,
fashions arose simply from people's desire to show their
affiliation with a certain cultural or ethnic group. As a
result of typical "pseudospecies" formation, the creation of various local costumes, particularly in mountain
valleys, has given rise to wonderful "species," "subspecies," and "local forms." On page 66 I have already

spoken of the relation of local costumes to collective aggression between groups. A second effect of fashion, more important for our present consideration, was first seen in larger town communities, where people began to demonstrate their rank by characteristic clothing. In his contribution to the symposium of the Institute of Biology in London, in 1964, James Laver, an authority on costume, showed that it was always people of higher rank who took care that the lower orders should not dress above their station. There is hardly an area of cultural history that so clearly expresses the increasing democratization of European countries as that of fashions in clothes.

In its original function, fashion probably had a stabilizing, conservative effect on cultural evolution. It was dictated by the patricians and aristocrats. As Otto Koenig has pointed out, the history of uniforms shows that ancient decorations, dating back to the age of chivalry and long since disappeared from soldiers' uniforms, for a long time continued to be worn as badges of the higher and top ranks. This premium on the older in fashion became inverted as soon as the consequences of neophilia (see page 40) made themselves felt. From then on, among a majority of people, it became a hallmark of status to be in the vanguard of all innovations. Obviously, it was in the interests of the mass producers to support the public opinion that it was good for the economy and for national growth to do so. Above all, they succeeded in convincing the great mass of consumers that ownership of the newest clothes, furniture, cars, washing machines, television sets, and so on, is the most infallible "status symbol." The silliest trifles were given the importance of status symbols and exploited by the manufacturers. As older car owners will remember, the hoods of earlier Buick models were endowed with completely unfunctional bull's-eye-shaped openings with chromium frames; the eight-cylinder models had three on each side, the cheaper six-cylinder ones only two. When, one day, the manufacturers started putting three bull's-eyes on the six-cylinder type also, sales of this model increased considerably, a fact that helped to offset the many angry letters written by eight-cylinder owners, protesting that the status symbol to which only their more expensive cars were entitled had been awarded to cars of inferior rank.

However, the worst effects of fashion and fad can be observed in the realm of science. It is a mistake to suppose that all professional scientists are free from the cultural diseases that are the subject of this treatise. Only the representatives of the immediately relevant sciences, the ecologists and psychiatrists, notice that something is amiss in the species Homo sapiens L., and it is these very scientists who are relegated by present-day public opinion to a very inferior status, as George Gaylord Simpson has so aptly described in "The Crisis in Biology," his satirical essay on the "pecking order" within the sciences.

Not only public opinion about science but also opinion within the scientific community tend to give pre-eminence to those sciences that are pre-eminent only from the point of view of a vulgarized society that has become alienated from nature, domesticated, cut off from traditional values and given to measuring solely in terms of commercial values. It is sad to see general opinion within the sciences afflicted with all the decay phenomena discussed in the preceding chapters. "Big Science" in no way implies a science concerned with the most important things on our planet, nor is it the science of the human psyche and intellect: it is exclusively that science which promises money, energy, or power, even if it is only the power destroying the really great and beautiful.

The primacy of physics among the sciences is not of man's making. In the system of the sciences, physics forms the basis. Every successful analysis, on every, even the highest integrational plane of natural systems, is a step "downward" to physics. Analysis means resolution, and what it resolves and eliminates is not the special laws of a more special science but only the borders of the next, more general one. A fully effective resolution of borders of this kind has only once succeeded: physical chemistry was able to reduce the natural laws of its subject to more general physical ones. In biochemistry, there are signs of an analogous resolution of the borders between biology and chemistry. Even if spectacular successes of this kind are hardly ever to be found in other sciences, the principle of analytical research is everywhere the same: we try to reduce the phenomena and laws of a field of knowledge, of a "stratum of real existence" (*Schichte des realen Seins*), as

Nicolai Hartmann, the philosopher, would say, to those prevailing in the nearest, more general field. To explain the workings of the higher system, we need to know these general laws, as well as the special structure of the system in which they take effect. We biologists consider the investigation and history of these structures important and difficult enough in themselves, and we do not agree with Crick that biology is a "rather simple extension of physics." We contend that physics, too, rests on a foundation, and that this foundation is a biological science, namely the science of the functioning human mind, in other words, epistemology. Nevertheless, we are good "physicalists," recognizing physics as the basis toward which our research is striving.

In my opinion, the fact that physics is generally recognized as the "pre-eminent" of sciences is due, not to the high esteem in which, as the basis of all the sciences, it is rightly held, but to other unpalatable factors already discussed in this book. As Simpson rightly says, the general public today thinks the less of a science, the higher, more complex and more valuable the object of its research. This can be explained only by the above-mentioned factors, as well as a few others that I will now discuss.

It is quite legitimate for a scientist to choose his research subject from any stratum of real existence on any integration level of life processes. Even the science of the human mind, particularly the theory of knowledge, is beginning to become a biological science. The so-called exactness of scientific research has nothing whatever to do with the complexity and the integration level of its subject; it is dependent only on the self-criticism of the scientist and the purity of his methods. To classify physics and chemistry as "exact sciences" is to insult all the others. Well-known sayings, such as that all research is science insofar as it involves mathematics, or that science consists in "measuring what is measurable, and making measurable what is not measurable," are epistemologically the greatest nonsense that ever came from the lips of those who should know better.

Although these pseudowise dicta are demonstrably false, their influence still dominates the picture of science. It is *fashionable* to make use of methods as physicslike as possible, irrespective of whether or not they promise success in the investigation of the particular object. Every science, including physics, begins with description, goes on to classification of the phenomena described and, only from there, to abstraction of the laws prevailing in them. Since the experiment serves the verification of the abstracted natural laws, thus it ranges last in the series of methods. These stages, called by Wilhelm Windelband, the philosopher, the descriptive, the systematic, and the nomothetic, must be gone through by every science. Since physics long ago arrived at the nomothetic and experimental stage, and since it has pressed so far into the nonvisualizable that it mostly has to define its objects after the operations by which it acquires knowledge of them, many people feel obliged to make use of these methods, even for the research objects that plainly require observation and description. The more complex and highly integrated an organic system is, the more strictly do we have to keep to the Windelband series of methods.

Thus, particularly in the field of behavior research, modern experimental operationalism applied at too early a stage produces the most paradoxical results. This fallacious procedure is supported by belief in the pseudodemocratic doctrine that the behavior of animal and man is determined, not by phylogenetically evolved structures of the central nervous system but exclusively by environmental influences and learning. The basic error in the thinking and working methods dictated by the behavioristic doctrine lies in this neglect of structures: all description of structure is considered superfluous, and only operational and statistical methods are regarded as legitimate. Since all biological laws result from the function of structures, it is hopeless to try to arrive at an abstraction of the laws governing the behavior of living beings, without descriptive investigation of their structure.

Easy though these elementary rules of science are to understand (they should be known to every student before he enters university), the fashion of simulating physics is asserting itself in nearly all branches of modern biology. The more complex the system under examination and the less we know about it, the more harmful this fashion is. The neurosensory system determining behavior in the higher animals and man can claim first place in both these respects.

The fashionable tendency to regard research on a lower integration level as "more scientific" easily leads to atomism, *i.e.*, to part examinations of subsystems without the obligatory consideration of the way in which these systems are integrated into the whole. The error in method does not lie in the attempt made by all research scientists to reduce life phenomena, even of highest integration levels, to basic natural laws and to explain them by these—in this sense we are all reductionists. The methodical error called reductionism lies in the fact that in this attempt at explanation we fail to consider the immeasurably complex *structure* into which the subsystems are integrated, and by which alone the systemic properties of the whole can be explained. Anyone wanting further information on the methodology of research that does justice to systems should read Nicolai Hartmann's *Aufbau der realen Welt* or Paul Weiss's essay "The Living System: Determinism Stratified." Both works say virtually the same; the fact that their subject is considered from very different viewpoints only makes the descriptions more graphic.

Just as clothes and car fashions do, modern scientific fashions achieve their worst effects by creating status symbols and, through these, the rank order in the sciences that Simpson has so derided. The modern operationalist, reductionist, quantificator, and statistician looks with contempt on all those old-fashioned scientists who believe they can acquire essential new insight into nature by observation and description of animal and human behavior, without experiments and even without mathematics. Research into highly integrated living systems is recognized as "scientific" only if, due to purposive measures (Donald Griffin aptly calls them simplicity filters), the structure-bound systemic properties give the deceptive impression of "exact," that is, physics-like simplicity: or, if the statistical evaluation of a numerically impressive data material makes us forget that the "elementary particles" under examination are human beings and not neutrons, in other words, only if all that is interesting in highly integrated organic systems, including that of man, is left out of consideration. This applies particularly to subjective experience, which, like something highly indecent, is repressed in the Freudian sense. If somebody makes his own subjective experience the subject of his investigation, he is accused of subjectivism, particularly if he dares to make use of the isomorphy of psychological and physiological processes as the source of knowledge for understanding them. The doctrinaires of the pseudodemocratic doctrine have apparently inscribed "psychology without psyche" on their banner, forgetting entirely that they themselves, in their most "objective" research, only acquire knowledge of the examined object by way of their own subjective experience. They consider anyone crazy who maintains that the study of the human mind can be pursued as a natural science.

All these errors of method are basically unscientific. They can be explained only as the results of the ideological pressure exerted by the consensus of larger, firmly indoctrinated human masses, a pressure which, in other areas of human life, too, is often capable of producing the most incredible fads. The special danger of fashionable indoctrination in the field of science lies in the fact that it leads too many, though fortunately not all modern scientists, in a direction exactly opposite

to that of the real aim of all human striving for truth—
the aim for better self-knowledge. In science, the trend
prescribed by present-day fashion is inhuman in the
worst sense of the word. Certain thinkers, who clearly
see the phenomena under discussion infiltrating humanity like malignant growths, incline to the opinion that
scientific thinking is, in itself, inhuman and that it has
brought on the danger of dehumanization. I am not of
this opinion. On the contrary, I believe that modern scientists, as children of their time, are afflicted by the
dehumanization symptoms that have sprung up primar-
ily in nonscientific cultures everywhere. Not only is
there a clear correlation between culture diseases in
general and those affecting science in particular, but,
on closer consideration, the former prove to be the cause
and not the effect of the latter. The dangerous, fashionable indoctrination of science, which is threatening to
rob humanity of its last supports, could never have come
about had its way not been paved by the cultural diseases treated in four of the earlier chapters of this book:
overpopulation with its unavoidable deindividualization
and uniformalization; alienation from nature with loss
of the ability to feel awe; man's commercial race
against himself, and his utilitarian way of thinking,
which turns the means into the end and forgets the
original aim; and last but not least, the general waning
of the emotions. All these bring on the dehumanizing
symptoms apparent in the sciences: they are their cause
and not their effect.

Nine

Nuclear Weapons

If we compare the threat to mankind by nuclear weapons with the dangers of the other deadly sins, we cannot deny that, of all the eight, it is the easiest to avert. Admittedly, an undiagnosed psychopath could gain access to the trigger button, or a simple accident could be mistaken by an opponent for an attack, unleashing havoc. Yet it is absolutely clear what we have to do against "the bomb"; we need not drop it or even make it. Because of the incredible collective stupidity of mankind, this is difficult enough to achieve; in the case of the other dangers, not even those who see them clearly know what to do about them. With regard to the dropping of the atom bomb, I am more optimistic that this will be prevented than that man's other seven sins will be checked.

The chief trouble caused today by the threat of nuclear weapons is the "Armageddon atmosphere" that it creates. The contemporary infantile striving for instant gratification and the corresponding inability to feel responsible for anything in the more distant future are certainly connected with the fact that at the subconscious root of all decisions lies the anxious question of how long, anyway, the world is going to exist.

Ten

Summary

I have discussed eight separate but causally connected processes that are threatening to destroy not only our civilization but mankind as a species.

These processes are:

1. Overpopulation of the earth which, because of the superabundance of social contacts, forces every one of us to shut himself off in an essentially "inhuman" way, and which, because of the crowding of many individuals into a small space, elicits aggression.

2. Devastation of our natural environment, with destruction not only of our surroundings but also of man's reverential awe for the beauty and greatness of a creation superior to him.

3. Man's race against himself, which pushes the development of technology to an ever faster pace, blinding people to all real values and robbing them of time for the genuinely human activity of reflection.

4. The waning of all strong feelings and emotion, caused by overindulgence. The process of technology and pharmacology furthers an increasing intolerance of

everything inducing the least unpleasure. Thus human beings lose the ability to experience a joy that is only attainable through surmounting serious obstacles. The natural waves of joy and sorrow ebb away into an imperceptible oscillation of unutterable boredom.

5. Genetic decay. In our modern civilization, apart from the "innate sense of justice" and a few transmitted traditions of right and wrong, there are no factors that exert a selection pressure tending to preserve instinctive norms of social behavior, although, with the growth of society, these are becoming more and more necessary. It is an alarming possibility that the many infantilisms are turning a certain type of hippie into social parasites.

6. The break in tradition. A critical point is reached at which the younger generation is no longer able to communicate with the older one, still less to identify with it. Therefore, the younger treats the older like an *alien ethnic group,* confronting it with the equivalent of national hatred. Hence, the continuance of tradition is threatened. The reasons for this disturbance are to be found principally in the lack of contact between parents and children, which even at the earliest stages of infancy can have pathological consequences.

7. Increased indoctrinability of mankind. The increase in numbers of people within a single cultural group, together with the perfection of technical means, lead to the possibility of maneuvering public opinion into a uniformity unprecedented in the history of mankind. Furthermore, the suggestive effect of an accepted doctrine grows with the number of its supporters, possi-

bly in geometric progression. There are cultures in which an individual who purposely keeps aloof from the influence of mass media, for example from television, is regarded as pathological. Deindividualizing effects are desired by all those whose intention it is to manipulate large bodies of people. Opinion polls, advertising, cleverly directed fads and fashions help the mass producers on this side of the iron curtain, and the functionaries on the other side to attain what amounts to a similar power over the masses.

8. The arming of mankind with nuclear weapons constitutes a threat easier to avert than the seven other developments described above.

The processes of dehumanization discussed in Chapters 2 to 8 give support to the pseudodemocratic doctrine which maintains that the social and moral behavior of man is in no way determined by the phylogenetically evolved organization of his nervous system and of his sense organs but, rather, that this behavior is determined solely by the "conditioning" to which, in the course of his ontogenesis, he is exposed by his particular cultural environment.

Bibliography

Bolk, L. *Das Problem der Menschwerdung.* Jena, 1926.

Campbell, D. T. "Pattern Matching as an Essential in Distal Knowing." In *The Psychology of Egon Brunswik,* edited by K. R. Hammond. New York: Holt, Rinehart and Winston, 1966.

Carson, R. *Silent Spring.* Boston: Houghton Mifflin, 1962.

Craig, W. "Appetites and Aversions as Constituents of Instincts." *Biological Bulletin,* 34, 1918.

Crick, F. *Of Molecules and Men.* Seattle: University of Washington Press, 1966.

Erikson, E. H. "Ontogeny of Ritualisation in Man." In *Philosophical Transactions, Royal Society,* London 251 B, 1966, pp. 337–349.

———. *Insight and Responsibility.* New York: Norton, 1964.

Gehlen, Arnold. *Der Mensch: Seine Natur und seine Stellung in der Welt.* Frankfurt: Athenäum Verlag, 1966.

Hahn, K. "Die List des Gewissens." In *Erziehung und Politik, Minna Specht zu ihrem 80. Geburtstag. Frankfurt* (Öffentliches Leben), 1960.

Hartmann, N. *Der Aufbau der realen Welt.* Berlin (de Gruyter), 1964.

Heinroth, O. *Beiträge zur Biologie, namentlich Ethologie und Psychologie der Anatiden.* Verhandlungen V. Internationaler Ornithologischer Kongress, Berlin, 1910.

Holst, E. v. "Über den Prozess der zentralnervösen Koordination." In *Pflügers Archiv.* 236, 1935, pp. 149–158.

————. "Vom Dualismus der motorischen und der automatisch-rhythmischen Funktion im Rückenmark und vom Wesen des automatischen Rhythmus." In *Pflügers Archiv*. 237, 1936, p. 3.

Huxley, A. *Brave New World*. New York: Harper & Row, 1932.

Koenig, O. *Kultur und Verhaltensforschung: Einführung in die Kulturethologie*. München: Deutscher Taschenbuchverlag, 1970.

Laver, J. "Costume as a Means of Social Aggression." In *The Natural History of Aggression*, edited by J. D. Carthy and F. J. Ebling. New York: Academic Press, 1965.

Leyhausen, P. "Über die Funktion der relativen Stimmungshierarchie. Dargestellt am Beispiel der phylogenetischen und ontogenetischen Entwicklung des Beutefangs von Raubtieren." In *Zur Tierpsychologie* 22, 1965, pp. 412–494.

Lorenz, K. "Psychologie und Stammesgeschichte." In *Die Evolution der Organismen*, edited by G. Heberer. Jena: Fischer, 1954.

————. *On Aggression*. New York: Harcourt Brace Jovanovich, 1966.

————. *Evolution and Modification of Behavior*. Chicago: University of Chicago Press, 1965.

————. *Studies in Animal and Human Behaviour*. Cambridge: Harvard University Press, 1970–71.

————. *Innate Bases of Learning*. Cambridge: Harvard University Press, 1969.

Mitscherlich, A. *Society Without the Father*. New York: Harcourt Brace Jovanovich, 1969.

Montagu, M. A. *Man and Aggression*. New York: Oxford University Press, 1968.

Popper, K. R. *The Logic of Scientific Discovery*. New York: Harper & Row, 1959.

Schulze, H. *Der progressiv domestizierte Mensch und seine Neurosen*. München: Lehmann, 1964.

———. *Das Prinzip Handeln in der Psychotherapie.* Stuttgart: Enke Verlag, 1971.

Simpson, G. G. "The Crisis in Biology," *The American Scholar* 36 (1967), pp. 363–377.

Spitz, R. A. *The First Year of Life.* New York: International Universities Press, 1965.

Vogt, W. *The Road to Survival.* New York: W. Sloane Associates, 1948.

Weiss, P. A. "The Living System: Determinism Stratified." In *Beyond Reductionism,* edited by A. Koestler and J. R. Smythies. London: Hutchinson, 1969.

Windelband, W. *Geschichte und Naturwissenschaft,* 1894.

Wylie, P. *The Magic Animal.* New York: Doubleday, 1968.

Wynne-Edwards, V. C. *Animal Dispersion in Relation to Social Behaviour.* New York: Hafner, 1962.